# THE BASIC IDEAS OF SCIENCE OF MIND

# THE
# BASIC IDEAS
# OF
# SCIENCE
# OF MIND

*by Ernest Holmes*

SCIENCE OF MIND PUBLICATIONS
Los Angeles, California

First Printing — June 1957


Twentieth Printing — February 1979

*Originally published as the 1957 Annual Edition of* Science
of Mind *Magazine under the title "An Introduction
to the Basic Ideas of Science of Mind"*

*Published by* SCIENCE OF MIND PUBLICATIONS
3251 West Sixth Street, Los Angeles, California 90020

# CONTENTS

# INTRODUCTION

THE AVERAGE MAN OR WOMAN of today feels the need of God in everyday life, an idea of God so rational that it appeals to the scientific mind of the modern person and enables him to see his way clearly in a universe which is run according to law and order. We all like to feel that we can depend on certain definite principles because our minds have been trained to know and understand the necessity for such a systematic basis as a foundation for our beliefs.

An intelligent thinker deeply desires a way of life which shows him how to be successful in his work, business, or profession, happily adjusted in his home and to his environment, strong and vigorous in body, and keen of mind.

Above all, he seeks something which will satisfy the hunger of his inmost nature — that longing for something steadfast and secure on which he can rely. Whether or not he admits it, he yearns for an understandable, permanent, and dependable relationship with God.

It is to meet these needs, which all mankind has in common, that this introduction to the basic ideas of Science of Mind has been written. No matter what your past or present circumstances, the application of these ideas will give you a new insight into your own inherent nature and will start you on such an intelligent, systematic, happy, and purposeful use of life that your experience will become wholesome and satisfying. You will learn the way to happiness, health, prosperity, and a more satisfactory way of living. Careful study and daily use of every suggestion given will richly repay you.

No one can do your growing for you, but you can learn *how to do that growing.*

ERNEST HOLMES

# CHAPTER I

## YOU AND YOUR MIND

EVERY HUMAN BEING thrills at the thought of achievement. The idea means different things to different people. To you it may mean physical health; the ability to walk, run, play, to engage in activity. To me, it may mean abundance; money, a home, a car — opulence. To another, achievement may mean education, or the ability to get along with people. Whatever achievement or happiness may mean to you, you desire a larger amount of it, a closer affiliation with it.

The ability to control your experiences and have them result in happiness, prosperity, and success lies in your own mind and the way you use it. This means you control your own experience — you are really in charge of your affairs and the way they are to develop.

Let us sum it up this way: *My thought is in control of my experience and I can direct my thinking.*

Read that again and then say it aloud. It is a most astounding statement and at first it may seem farfetched. But because you are a modern person with an open mind ready to be shown what you may not at first understand — even what does not seem entirely believable — you will be willing to take that statement under consideration and hear the reasons for it. Certainly you do not have to believe it, and you do not wish to until you have investigated it, heard the arguments in its favor, and observed whether or not it works for you after you have given it a fair trial. That is the way the intelligent mind approaches any new idea.

### INTELLECTUAL INVESTIGATION

No one can thrust any new belief upon another; no one has

any right to attempt to do so. It is only when we have made the right intellectual inquiries and investigations for ourselves that we can honestly decide whether to accept or reject what is presented to us. We are not going to allow ourselves to be coerced into anything of which our own good judgment does not approve. However, we cannot bring our good judgment to bear upon anything, in fullest measure, until we have been fair in our efforts to understand and then faithful in our attempts to test it to see if it actually does work for us. This is only reasonable.

If you have been brought up under Christian influences in the home and church you will feel particularly sensitive about your religion and inclined to say, "I do not want anything which will disturb my faith in God as an Overruling Providence and in Jesus as the wayshower for men through his practical application of a loving, useful life and his triumphant conquest even over death itself."

In response we say, "You are exactly right!"

On the other hand, if you have lived apart from church activities and associations, or have found them unfitted to your scientific turn of mind, and you want something on which you can base your thinking and faith that retains a clear concept of the orderly world of science in which natural laws and order prevail, then we say, "That is a rational viewpoint and we believe you will find much that is of interest and value to you."

Possibly, though, you may be just a busy man or woman desirous of a wholesome, successful life and a sense of security. If you are to give your attention to anything new in the way of thinking, it will have to be something you can apply in your everyday affairs, and which you can know will work!

This is a good sensible way to look at it.

If there is an understanding of God that meets your daily needs in a world of practical affairs, you want it. If there is some system of reasoning which conforms to your keenest intellectual rationalization and scientific knowledge, it is of interest to you. If you can find something that will satisfy that deep inner hunger which lies in the hearts of all, whether they ever acknowledge it or not, you are just as eager as anyone else to find that satisfaction. You have practical daily needs that must be met; intellectual demands which seek rational fulfillment, and sincere spiritual longings that have to be fulfilled. This is true of all persons; you are no exception.

## YOUR PERSONAL IMPORTANCE

Now that we have a foundation for mutual understanding and a willingness to look into this way of thinking, let us go back to our earlier statement, enlarge it, and give it more careful consideration:

> *The ability to control my experiences and have them result in happiness, prosperity, and success lies in my own mind and my use of it.*

In the field of physical science it has been proved that absolutely everything can be scientifically reduced to one ultimate invisible Essence, something which cannot be contacted by the physical senses. It is therefore only reasonable to say that originally everything must have, and still does, come from It. According to one's way of thinking, different names are given to It: Energy, Principle, Universal Intelligence, Universal Mind, Consciousness, Spirit, God.

For our purpose it does not particularly matter which of these names we use. Let us call It *Mind*. This probably has the broadest meaning for most of us, without too many limiting ideas connected with it.

## YOU ARE ONE WITH EVERYTHING IN THE UNIVERSE

Scientists show us that Energy — an aspect of Mind — is interchangeable with substance, and is everywhere; within us, around us, filling all space to the limitless reaches of the universe.

Everything we can see, touch, taste, smell, or contact in any physical way, we are told, is but some aspect of this Universal Energy or Mind which has been channeled into specific and tangible form so that our senses become aware of It. For instance, on a summer day, entirely invisible vapor arises from the ocean and soars high in the sky. By contact with a different air temperature it becomes a dainty cloud. If colder air still further condenses it, it turns into raindrops which help to fill a lake. In winter a still further change takes place and instead of raindrops there are snow crystals. Winter also changes the water of the lake to ice. In every instance we have only that original vapor which has taken a form of which our senses are aware. This is but a very simple example.

It was Einstein's famous equation, $E = MC^2$, which revolutionized and clarified much scientific thinking and at the same time cleared the way for the establishing of firmer foundations for considerable philosophical and religious thought. In essence it means that energy and mass (that which has physical qualities) are one and the same and are interchangeable. From our point of view this would mean that Mind — God — acting as Energy becomes what we know as the physical world, according to Law. They are one and the same thing, but God being infinite could never be depleted by what is created. It is only reasonable to declare that everything which is ever to be must also come from God. In fact there is nothing else out of which anything could be made.

Mind is everywhere! After all, this is just the same as saying what we were taught to say in earliest childhood: "God is everywhere." That statement did not mean much to us then, but now we know that this Universal Mind is everywhere. Therefore It is within us!

There can be no exception to this *everywhere-ness*. This gives us the key to the whole situation, and makes us understand that not only our individual minds, but our bodies as well, are expressions and a part of Mind.

## HOW TO UTILIZE THIS UNITY

At the beginning of this world system of ours there must have been nothing but the great Universal Mind — God — and out of Itself the tangible universe was formed.

We were taught the omnipresence of God — Universal Mind — and also that we were made in His image and likeness. So we arrive at the conclusion that *we, too, at our level, possess a creativity similar to that of the Universal Mind.* We create in our experience whatever we choose: health, happiness, prosperity, employment — any good thing we need — through the process of our constructive thought, through which the unlimited Creativity of Mind acts, giving form to our desired objective. You are a *vital part* of this harmonious Universe.

It appears from experience that the only way for the individual to constructively use the Creativity of this invisible, but everywhere-present Mind, is by means of his thought — faith and conviction — and nothing else.

## OUR RIGHT TO CREATE

Today the old idea of our being like God, the image-and-likeness concept, applies in a new and different but very important way. Since we are created of that which God is — Mind — we are made of and possess God-like qualities and we have the right and the ability to develop and use them. In fact it is necessary for us to do this if we are to fully express the Life within us.

Later we shall discuss these qualities, but just now we are interested in the creative aspect of our minds. There is created for us what we *choose*, out of and through the action of the One Universal Mind, which is everywhere and is accessible to us.

You avail yourself of the Creative Action of Mind through what you believe! Perhaps you are not quite ready to accept this statement, but it is an interesting one, and one that is well worth remembering.

## HOW CAN WE LEARN TO BELIEVE?

First of all, you must remember that you can think what you please. No one can direct your thought processes. They are under your own control.

Someone may say, "You must think as a Republican," or "You have to be a Democrat in your thinking," or "My church's way of religious thinking is the only right one, that is what you have to think," or "When you see a blackboard you have to think of its being white." All of this is ridiculous. You may have to make your *actions* conform to what those in authority tell you, but they simply cannot control your *thinking*. You will go on thinking just as you want to. In that respect you are independent, no matter where you live.

If your thinking processes are really under your personal control, as you will agree that they must be, and if thought is acted upon by the Creativity of Mind producing results according to your belief, then you surely do have the power to become the master of your own affairs and to bring to pass those good conditions you desire.

This makes the *omnipresence of God* and the *made in the image and likeness of God* very practical and important ideas rather than abstract theological concepts. They can now become outstanding truths which belong to your everyday life and are therefore of prime importance in all the practical aspects of living.

Let us keep in mind that we not only have the God-given ability to do this kind of resultful thinking, but that we also have the right to do it. In connection with the God-Power within you, there are many other aspects, but this one — *the right and the ability and power to "think creatively" so that you have more desirable experiences* — is so impressive and so exceedingly important that it should be the basis of your life. Even though you may not fully accept or understand this statement as yet, you can begin to put it into actual application for yourself. You can start right now to make it work!

### HE TRIED IT!

A true story is told of a man in one of our Eastern cities who a few years ago had been in one position for twenty-five years, at a very mediocre salary. He had become extremely dissatisfied, wanted to get out of the rut, but didn't know how to do it. When he accepted a few simple, but profound, ideas like these he began to realize that within himself he had the right and ability to declare better conditions for himself. In less than one month from the time he began to think in this way — and to act accordingly — his salary was increased to exactly three times what it had been before!

When we get only a glimpse of the true nature of Mind — the God-Power within us — and use It, the results are truly amazing. Physically, financially, socially, intellectually, and spiritually it pays us to learn and to use the principles of creative thinking. The laboratory student who tries a valid experiment and fails, does not give up; he tries again and again until he proves it for himself. Shouldn't we be equally faithful in testing these scientific laws? Our personal welfare demands continued and faithful endeavor and experimentation.

There is but One Mind; It is Omnipresent — It is all there is. Everything, visible and invisible, is but a manifestation of this One Mind — the result of Its Creative Action and the becoming of that which It creates.

Because you are made in the image and likeness of God, you can use your mind, according to its nature, and, by choice, bring your good to you. Keep yourself aware of the truth that *everything is some aspect of Mind.*

Now examine the diagram (next page) and think of it as representing the entire universe, all that is. All of it is Mind. For the sake of clarity we divide it into three sections, but it is all Mind!

Part I we may call Conscious Mind. Automatically you think of your conscious mind as being that faculty with which you think and plan. With it you become aware of ideas, analyze,

# *MIND · GOD · INTELLIGENCE · SPIRIT*

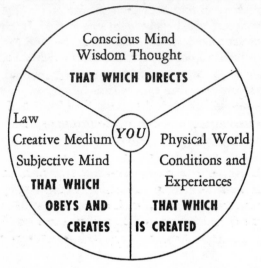

make decisions, and carry on all mental processes. Let us think of it as the superintendent of a manufacturing plant, who thinks out what is to be done and gives instructions. Needless to say, nothing could be accomplished if there were not some department to take those instructions and carry them out.

Part II is the part of Mind that obeys the directions of Part I. Think of it as the factory where the instructions are taken and worked out. We call this the Subjective Mind, the Law which acts and creates automatically according to instructions. It is obedient to the directions of Part I. Without Part I it would be useless for lack of instructions. Without Part II, Part I would be helpless for want of something to take directions and bring them to fulfillment. One part, therefore, is just as important as the other.

Now look at Part III and realize that this is the only part of the universe you can experience — see, touch, or contact with your physical senses — the realm of tangible things and conditions. Here are the results of what was directed by Part I and carried out by Part II. I and II instigate and carry out; III is the result or effect.

In the diagram see the tiny portion marked "You." Notice that you, too, possess the three aspects of Mind: direction, creation, result.

Remember:

1. Everything is Mind and you are therefore a part of It.

2. Mind responds and produces according to *your* believing thought.

3. You have the right and power to think what you want to think; therefore you may create desired good conditions for yourself and others.

4. You control your own good and may transform your life into an experience of happiness, health, and prosperity.

# CHAPTER II

## YOUR THINKING AND HEALTH

THE FIRST THING you should do at this point is to realize that you *can* achieve health through right thinking. A state of expectancy is a great asset. A state of uncertainty — one moment of thinking "perhaps" and the next moment thinking "I don't know" — will never get desired results. Even God can give you nothing until you make up your mind what it is you expect.

The principle involved may be summed up in the words: *Mind responds to mind.* It is done unto you as you believe. Therefore our bodily conditions are governed by our thought processes. This idea is now corroborated by psychosomatic medicine.

In order to understand this principle so that you can apply it, refer to the diagram at the end of the last chapter. We called Part I the conscious mind, that aspect of Mind in us with which we do our thinking and reasoning. From time to time reference may be made to the expression "objective mind." Do not be confused; this is only another way of referring to what we have called the conscious mind.

We referred to Part II as the subjective mind. Subjective means "under the direction of" and this is true concerning that portion of Mind which acts as Law — the creative, obedient, formative Power. It does not mean that it is any less important. We need always to remember that there is but One Universal Mind. Each one of us uses a portion of It. Really, each one of us *is* a portion of It, for all — everything — is Mind. By designating Its different activities we find it a little easier to understand the way It works and to be able to use It more intelligently.

### *AUTOMATIC PROTECTION*

In considering the creation of health by right thinking we

also need to realize that it is through Law that the body is built and maintained. Basically It is constantly at work sustaining God's perfect idea of man. It keeps us breathing, keeps our hearts beating, takes care of our temperature, circulates the blood, digests our food, eliminates refuse, and does everything which keeps the marvelously intricate machinery of the body in operation. It is far wiser than any chemist in the world and is forever at work. It never sleeps, and in our sleep the Law carries on all our physical needs and gets us into good condition for the activities of the waking hours that are to come.

## THE VALUE OF HABIT

There is a second way, however, in which Law is of exceedingly great value. A habit is the result of something we have done with careful attention and conscious effort so many times that we do not now have to think specifically about it when doing it. That is, the Law of Mind responds to a persistent idea and automatically maintains it. This we call habit. We can talk and walk and do scores of different kinds of work and play and still be thinking of other things. But we could not do so at first. We had to form persistent thought patterns before these activities could be released from our conscious attention. Certainly we owe a vast debt of gratitude to that obedient Law of Mind in action. In thousands of ways It is eminently wise. It does many things we could not possibly know enough about to direct It in the doing.

In the matter of habits, though, when we have found that this very accommodating and capable function of Mind will accept any thought pattern we persistently give to It, and will from then on automatically maintain it for us, it is only reasonable and wise for us to give over into Its care those things which would be advantageous to us. There are many attitudes and activities in which we ought to be more proficient, which would make us more agreeable companions, more capable workers, happier individuals — more skillful, adaptable, and efficient. We can be more healthy and more prosperous and can advance our own welfare in many ways by simply deciding what it is we desire to be, or to do, and then giving the matter enough conscious attention so that it becomes a habitual thought pattern — that is, the Law of Mind maintaining it for us. The Law of Mind is obedient to conscious direction.

## WATCH YOUR MENTAL ATMOSPHERE

This is one of the great, important, and valuable ways in which our thought works:

*Mind responds to mind.*

Mind is intelligence, and of course intelligence responds to intelligence.

We can put this principle into operation in regard to our health, either to prevent illness, or to heal it after it has developed. We all know that in the process of living millions of body cells are being replaced daily. Millions of new cells are constantly growing within our bodies, and they immediately take on the atmosphere of the surroundings in which they find themselves. The atmosphere or tone of the body may be considered as wholesome, happy, optimistic, and therefore healthy, or the opposite — gloomy, apprehensive, frightened, fearful, anxious, discouraged, and weak and sickly. This atmosphere is the sum total of the way we are allowing ourselves to think and feel. It may be that we are really ill. If so, it is especially necessary that we give today's new cells the right, wholesome, happy atmosphere in which to live and work, for by doing so we get at least that much of our system into good order. If we can maintain that right mental atmosphere, tomorrow's new cells added to today's supply will bring us that much nearer recovery.

Scientists now assert that in only eleven months *all the cells* of the body are made new. So, day after day in thought we can add to our experience of wholesomeness and health, and in this way redeem the whole body from illness. There is ample medical proof as to the effect of sad, gloomy, anxious thoughts upon the general welfare and the functions of the body, and also as to the healing power of right thinking. This is nothing we need to take on blind faith; it is scientific knowledge.

## WATCH YOUR THOUGHTS

The beliefs which we have accepted — to which Law automatically responds — are continually being brought forth into our experience. The results are good health or illness, depending upon what we have believed. Because of this principle and our understanding of it, we can keep ourselves well and happy, and free of disease; or, if we have become ill, we can bring about the necessary healing. If this way of thinking did nothing else for us, it would be an unspeakably great blessing.

So far, though, we have been considering this from a very narrow viewpoint. It is as though we were keeping ourselves in that small circle in the diagram. We need to remember that it actually does not exist, there is no barrier between ourselves and the Universal Mind, God. Let us remember that each one is not separated from, but is a definite, distinct, and particular expression of God, an individualization of God, and has access to the whole of God-Wisdom and Power! In order for us to bring to pass any specific result, there has to be a particular pattern or thought through which it may manifest. Your thinking is the mold of your experience. The Unlimited, Universal Mind in you as you thinks and speaks and creates your *good* through you — when you are wise enough to permit It. Now you can declare your own health because you know you are of the Infinite. You may be assured of perfect results because what is termed your mind is an individualization of the One Mind and possesses Its creativity. That All-wise and All-powerful Mind flows creatively through you and can by means of your believing thought fulfill your needs and supply a greater experience of good.

## EXAMPLES OF RIGHT THINKING

Anyone who observes carefully will soon accumulate much

evidence to prove that bodily illness is produced by wrong thinking and that it can be healed by right thinking.

The *British Medical Journal* says: "There is not a tissue in
the human body wholly removed from the influence of the
spirit."

Dr. Adrian Taylor, Chief Surgeon and Superintendent of
the Clifton Springs Sanitorium at Clifton Springs, New York,
said: "A large majority of the surgical cases that come to me
should never really have come. They could have been headed
off ... Wrong moral and mental attitudes created functional
disturbances in the physical organism and these in turn became
organic or structural disease. At this point I get them as a surgeon, but they could have been headed off by the kind of Christ-
ianity presented here." (He refers to the principles set forth in
the book, *Is the Kingdom of God Realism?* by E. Stanley Jones,
in which Dr. Jones stresses the importance of right thinking for
the maintenance of health.)

E. A. Strecker, in his book *Mental Hygiene* said: "Fully 50%
of the problems of the acute stages of illness and 75% of the
difficulties of convalescence have their primary origin not in the
body, but in the mind of the patient."

Dr. Franz Alexander, of the Institute of Psycho-Analysis in
Chicago, said: "Hostility, suppressed for years, like a boiling
volcano which never erupts, is the fundamental cause of malig-
nant high blood pressure for which no physical cause has ever
been found."

One doctor tells of a woman who greatly disliked her son-
in-law, yet for the sake of seeing her daughter she visited in
their home once each year. Every time she went she suffered
from arthritis; after coming away from his hated presence she
recovered.

Hundreds of such examples could be given, but they do us
very little good if we do not prove the principle for ourselves.
The Law of Mind in action manifests for us the beliefs we
speak into It. When we understand there is a definite Law with
which we are working, it is much easier to have the faith re-
quired to bring healing. Remember, we are spiritual beings.
The real "I," our special individuality, is God in us as us, and
as such must of course be perfect. This "I" functions through

the intellect, the emotions, and the body — all parts of one indivisible Whole.

## IDEAS FOR YOU

The following simple procedures practiced daily in a persistent, happy, and expectant manner, will soon produce a good effect upon your health:

Night and morning try to set apart a time in which to be quiet, to commune with your *real* self. This is really the period in which you clarify your mental atmosphere. Be as relaxed physically as you can, but neither the position you occupy, the chair in which you sit, nor the room has anything to do with the work you are doing. Merely see to it that there is no physical discomfort while you are attempting to direct your thinking.

Now that some of the bodily tenseness, which is the bane of our rushing way of living, has been released, say with conviction and feeling:

*I am strong and free through the Action of God in me.*

*I am well and successful in everything I do.*

Repeat this until you feel the thrill of it all through you. It is a wonderful tonic.

After this spend ten minutes thinking over some part of what you have read, assimilating it more, or have a quiet prayer time in which you do not *ask* for things or conditions, but name them, *accept* them as already belonging to you, and give *thanks* for them.

## BE GOOD TO YOUR BODY

This whole procedure has probably taken about twenty minutes. You would not start on a day's trip in your car without an adequate supply of gas and oil. Why start out on your day's work without getting yourself properly supplied, physically, emotionally, and spiritually?

A feeling of complete well-being will diffuse through you at the conclusion. See if you cannot keep this high consciousness all day.

Even if it should not seem to mean much to you the first day or so, keep at it. This is a process of changing your whole way of life and it requires the re-education of your body, your emotions, your intellect, and your spiritual outlook. Be fair to yourself. Keep on!

Plant deeply in your mind these four basic ideas:

1. You are completely surrounded by and are part of Mind. It interpenetrates your very being; It is what you are.

2. This Mind is always creative, manifesting what you think and believe as form or some experience.

3. Mind answers to mind. Mind creates for you according to the pattern you make for It — by your clearly defined thoughts of good — if you *believe* It will.

4. Because of this you can choose to remain in good health, or to be healed if you are now ill. In the same manner you may choose and bring into your experience any other good condition.

To declare yourself into good health is one of the greatest blessings you could ever enjoy. The simple explanations given here are to start you on the way to the making of such declarations, because you can now begin to understand what it is that is needed in order to bring healing about.

# CHAPTER III

## YOUR THINKING AND FINANCES

ARE YOU INTERESTED in making money? In running your business successfully? In getting a better salary? Of course you are! You want to be prosperous, and this is only right and sensible.

The plain, practical, everyday problem of money-making is a definite part of living and the answer to it is summed up in these words: *Prosperity awaits man's recognition and acceptance of it.* Or it can be stated another way: Your financial success already exists, but it is waiting for you to see it and accept it as your own.

So far we have discovered that we are surrounded by limitless Mind — Energy — out of which everything is made. Also, it is the nature of the Universe to always take form according to a pattern, through the process of Law. Through our belief and conviction we provide patterns for Its manifestation. It is often helpful to realize that the Universe is infinite and that we can always draw on It for any desired good, that there is no limit to the good that can be manifest. When we say It "awaits man's recognition" we mean that as soon as we intellectually understand the nature of the unseen part of our Universe and the way It works, and wholeheartedly believe in It, then we can more effectively use It.

### USE YOUR BANK ACCOUNT

If someone told you that he had placed a thousand dollars to your credit in a certain bank, but you did not believe it, it would do you no good even though you were in great need. The money could lie there, idle and useless, even though you starved to death. Even if you did believe it, but did nothing to make use of it, it still would do you no good. It would be sensible for you to go to the bank, prove your identity, get a checkbook, and begin to draw on that account.

So it is with this principle we desire to use. Not even your intelligent understanding of the accessibility and the limitless nature of infinite Creativity will be of any advantage to you unless you make proper use of it.

Learn to draw on your spiritual bank account! Please keep clearly in mind that it is spiritual — that everything is Spirit, Mind, God, either visible or invisible. Remember the vapor which changed to ice? Every tangible thing you see or possess or contact in any way is but an expression of Spirit manifesting according to a pattern.

If you need more money, it merely means that you need to place your order in this Cosmic Storehouse to have a greater supply of good become tangible in your experience.

It is important that you identify yourself with that greater financial supply which you desire. You cannot do this by thinking about it as though it were impossible or even unlikely, or regretting that you do not now have it. Instead, you must train yourself to think about it with a feeling that it is only reasonable and natural for it to be yours — yes, that it already *is* yours! The money we spoke about being in the bank is yours even though you may not have checked on it yet. You do not have to stop and argue with yourself about its value or accessibility. The essence of the All-surrounding Universal Mind becomes your experience according to the pattern you choose. If you choose money, then money it will be!

## BELIEVE YOUR GOOD IS AVAILABLE

It would be well worth your while to devote some time from your regular routine in order to get yourself into a mental state of *real* belief in this spiritual bank account of yours. Just as soon as you truly *believe* and *feel* with your whole being that your good is available, accept it, know it is yours, then it *is* yours!

When you believe a good is yours, the Universe has no choice but to respond to that belief.

This is a process of identification. You not only believe in your financial welfare, but you act as though it is *now* yours. With a good bank account you certainly are not going to act impoverished. Of course not; you will think, appear, and act prosperous. Your every attitude will indicate that you are financially successful for you have identified yourself with prosperity — a result that is only natural and inevitable. Anyone who sees you will immediately get this impression. Some will act this way only when they have a thousand dollars in the bank. Surely, you can act accordingly when you know you have access to the Universal Storehouse which is limitless.

## MAKING SOLID YOUR FOUNDATIONS

To make your financial welfare concrete, that is, to bring it out of the invisible realm of Cause into the visible, tangible realm of your experience, there are certain steps you need to take:

First of all, you must consistently *believe* in it. When you actually *expect* it you are well on the way to meeting it halfway. True expectancy is the highest test of faith.

Next, you need to know that you have the right and ability to declare financial success for yourself — to accept the Creative Action of Mind in this particular way — and also to know that you have practical skills and abilities that can be translated into the good that people want and will gladly pay for. The wise man never declares his oncoming good and then sits idly by waiting for it to arrive. No, he uses every bit of his knowledge, initiative, and skill — the Action of God in him — to make himself so useful and valuable that financial rewards automatically flow to him.

Some may be sorely in need of money and have no place to work where they can earn those much-needed funds. If this is your case, continue to look about you for opportunities, but do that only as a secondary matter. Your big task is to understand the Activity of Mind and your creative use of It. Believe in It, declare into It, and accept the answer. Know that your order has been received and is being filled. With this firmly implanted in your mind you are rightly guided when you look for work, for ways to increase your business, for greater outlets for your skill, or whatever other good you may desire. In this way you can act with a mind free of anxiety.

## EXPRESSION THROUGH SERVICE

If, at the start, you are not successful in finding the desired employment, new plans, or that which you have specifically wanted, then be very sure that you fill at least a portion of your time with some kind of outgiving service which will be of help to others. It is positively necessary that you be expressing yourself in some kind of worthy endeavor, because Life is action, and you must be creative in some respect. You may be greatly surprised to find that kind, generous, free service may be just the thing to set in motion the activities which will result in the position you need, the increased business, or your desired good!

The same is true in regard to the giving of money. It returns augmented with a certainty and promptness that is astonishing! There are hundreds of great needs in the world today where every dollar you can spare will serve some worthy purpose. You should not give carelessly, but when you know of a truly fine work which is being carried on and which needs your support, you do yourself an injustice if you do not contribute to it. Whether your cash on hand is large or small, what you take from it to give to others temporarily seems to deplete your supply — it leaves a vacuum. It is trite to say that "Nature abhors a vacuum," but it is a principle of vital importance to us in this connection. When you intelligently and generously give from what you have for the good of others, you may depend upon it that there will be a spiritual response, and concrete good will come rushing back to fill that empty space.

## A RICH CONSCIOUSNESS

Whether your funds be great or small, you need to get all possible pleasure and satisfaction out of them. This cannot be the case if you are fearful about spending. If you count too carefully, if you limit yourself unduly, because you do not know how you may be situated later on, you are restricting your good. If you are to be rich in concrete ways you must first be rich in consciousness, and have the *feeling* of abundance.

Common sense will guide your expenditures at all times, but get all the happiness and satisfaction you can out of every dollar you spend. If you are paying rent, buying clothes, or food — anything — you are using your money to get something you would rather have than that money, else you would not use it in that way. Be glad about it. Never, never hand over your money in payment for anything, grudgingly! If your best judgment advises a purchase, make it a transaction of mutual good will, be it great or small. The habit of silently blessing your money as you hand it over is worth cultivating. Then it carries with it an intangible value which will bring back good. Learn to bless your bills as you pay them, they indicate the good you have received and express the faith others have in you.

## WISH GREATLY FOR YOURSELF

You may wish very much to use money for some particular purpose but wonder if it is right to do so. "Am I selfish in using my money for this?" you ask. Use this test: "Will it be of value to me, and because of it will I be of greater help, inspiration, encouragement, or practical help to others? If so, it is right. If through me a greater good can come to others, this will be money wisely spent."

If it is something that will start you in a new and worthy service, even though it is your last dollar, use it freely and happily. Several years ago, in a large Midwest city, a young woman with a baby and an invalid husband took her last five dollars — her total capital — and with it made a first payment on a secondhand mimeograph. She bought on faith and with high hopes of making money to keep the family going. Because of the care of husband and child, she could not leave home for work. In odd hours, she went from house to house in the neighborhood, as well as in some business areas, and distributed mimeographed sheets listing different ways in which she could meet people's needs. Work began to come in almost immediately and the little business grew. To bravely step out and do what you can, with calm faith, having made your claim on Universal Creativity, and then acting intelligently, will bring the financial abundance desired.

## THE RIGHT TO SUCCESS

Science of Mind is a way of thinking which gives you an awareness of spiritual principles on which you may rely. It shows you how to use the Law of Mind, how to think effectively, or pray affirmatively, for what you need so that your life becomes wholesome, fine, successful, and good. Your prayers are always answered if they are declared in sincerity, believed in, and acted upon with common sense and in practical ways. You have a perfect right to use the creativity of your mind to provide abundant finances for a fuller, richer experience in living.

Are you eager for success? Ask yourself very candidly, "What have I done to merit it? Have I put my very best efforts into my work? Have I developed something new and unique in the service I offer or the business I carry on? Have I made myself especially proficient in some one particular and am I capitalizing on it? Do I honestly think how best to meet the needs of those with whom I do business so that they are most benefited? Can I see things from their viewpoint and adapt myself? Am I constantly improving my skill, my methods, and my personality? What have I done to earn my desired success?"

## CULTIVATE YOUR TALENT

Jesus made plain in his parable of the talents, the necessity of using what we possess. A man gave to one servant five talents; to another, two; and to another, one. On his return he called for the money and a report as to how it had been used. It must have been with considerable pride and satisfaction that the five-talent man could report he had doubled his money! So had he of the two talents. They had used good judgment and energetic activity. They had not wasted time by idly wishing the money were theirs, but had utilized their time to a good purpose. And so they had passed the test and were given positions of great honor and responsibility because in small ways they had proved their initiative, willingness, reliability, and business acumen. The man who made no practical use of what he had — his one talent — found, upon the master's return, that even it was taken from him. It is a good lesson for all of us to consider. Ask yourself again, "What have I done to earn my success?"

To achieve your desired prosperity you must:

*First,* understand there is an Unlimited Supply of all things which surrounds you; know that you have a right to draw on It; believe in the response which It always gives; and, then, believingly state your desire and accept the answer. This enables you to get rid of all anxiety about money and supply.

*Second,* whatever you can do objectively must be done enthusiastically and energetically. This is your part in bringing about your prosperity. When you have declared your good you must not try to figure out *how* it is to come. That is for Universal Mind to decide, and It is entirely capable of doing so. Never question *how*; just *know* It does, and that It works intelligently.

Remember:

1. Recognize the truth that Universal Abundance surrounds you.
2. Understand and believe in the responsiveness of the One Mind.

3. Know your right and ability to speak your word, believingly, and that the Activity of Mind as Law will manifest the good you choose.

4. Declare your good and *know* it is made manifest. Let there be no doubt or worry.

5. Act in every practical way you can. Life is action.

### LAYING FOUNDATIONS FOR PROSPERITY

*I am prospered because I believe in my prosperity.*
*I accept the responsiveness of the Universe.*

The more you make such statements, sincerely believing in them, cultivating a feeling of joy, and accepting them as true, knowing your perfect right and ability to do so, and realizing that Universal Mind is bringing them to pass, the more fully you will be laying the foundation for that prosperity you desire. *Unto everyone that hath shall be given.*

# CHAPTER IV

## REBUILDING YOUR LIFE

IT IS TIME TO CONSIDER a larger concept and attain a higher spiritual understanding of what you have read so far. You have learned something about what we may call the structure of Universal Mind, and of your relationship to It. You have caught a glimpse of how you may make use of that knowledge to bring about good health and financial success for yourself.

However, there is a great spiritual Law which applies to a vastly wider range of subjects, and which can apply to everything in life. One way it may be stated is: *Man, as a son of God, inherits the qualities and powers of the Father.*

To substantiate this we have the words of Jesus: " . . . for one is your Father, which is in heaven." " . . . and all ye are brethren." "For as the Father hath life in himself, so hath he given to the Son to have life in himself." Further confirmation is to be found in many other religions, in philosophy, as well as in the conclusions arrived at by many modern scientists.

Through eons of time life has been slowly climbing up the ladder of unfoldment to the present self-conscious state achieved in man. Some degree of consciousness exists in everything because everything is some form of Spirit, and Spirit is Intelligence. However, there are degrees of intelligence, or consciousness. We often hear the expression, "Consciousness sleeps in mineral life, dreams in plant life, awakens in animal life, and comes to self-consciousness in man." Man, then, stands at the very peak of the evolutionary climb. He is now a self-conscious individual which means that he not only knows, but knows that he knows. He can think about his own consciousness, and he now has the power of choice — the very summit of life's upward striving. Evolution, through infinite ages, has done much for him.

Now, however, if the individual is to continue to progress he must take things in his own hands and choose to continue his climb. From now on he ascends because he himself has chosen to do so. In order to do this one must clearly realize that there is no separation between man and God. Remember, *all is Spirit*, expressions of the infinite God-Consciousness. There is nothing in the Universe that can hinder your upward climb — your increased awareness of Oneness with God — nothing unless you decide not to climb any more. The vast expanse of an ever-widening upward reach is available to you.

## DESIRE AND WORK FOR THE BEST

In order to promote such growth you need to recognize the highest qualities in the range of human understanding, and cultivate them. Because all are sons of God it stands to reason that each has inherited the Father's qualities, and they already lie within, waiting to be recognized and developed. Your own logical reasoning makes it plain that if you are to live a highly successful and happy life you need to be able to express those innate abilities which will produce experiences and conditions of success and happiness. If those God-given abilities are to be specifically used by you, you need to know about their nature and source.

The statement of Jesus that the Father's life is in the son surely implies that the son must grow into the qualities of the Father in order to avail himself of that greater potential. You want to live wholesomely, successfully, and fill a worthy place in the world. If you are to do so you need to get acquainted with the characteristics that make up that kind of life, and then get to work and cultivate them.

## TRUE TO YOUR INNER DIVINITY

Each one of us might think of himself as an outlet through

which the activity of Spirit may flow. In fact, it is only as the qualities of God do flow through us that we more fully partake of His Nature, and that, after all, is our task — to more fully express the Nature of God, the Father. In whatever degree the qualities of perfection are part of your general conduct, to just that degree are you making God known to mankind. You are being true to your sonship only insofar as your inheritance of the Father's Nature is portrayed by you. Each has the privilege and the responsibility of being a clear channel for the flow of God through him, as him.

What, then, are these qualities which must be ours? Read the list and consider it carefully. Unless all of these are experienced fully in your life, you need to become more aware of your unity with God. The God-qualities are an integral part of you; they lie deep within you, whether you admit it or not. At the center of your being are Life, Love, Wisdom, Intelligence, Peace, Creativity, Beauty, and Joy.

Immediately you realize that if all persons made use of these qualities — actually lived them — there could be no inharmony, no lack, no ignorance, no illness, no sordidness, fear, or sadness. For growth into our God-like nature Jesus proclaimed "the way, the truth, and the life." It is to this high consciousness that we aspire, and as it unfolds within us these qualities are developed. What Jesus did, we, too, must do. We have no reason not to fully believe and accept his amazing statement: ". . . the works that I do shall he do also; and greater works than these shall he do . . . "

You honestly do want to accomplish and achieve to that which shall produce for you the wholesome, happy, and successful life — the joyous, healthy life — which your awareness of the Nature of God holds out for you. To aspire and attain to this you must recognize that you have, by nature, the requisite ability within and then cultivate those qualities which will let it develop.

## YOUR INFINITE POSSIBILITY

The first step is an awareness that you *already are* the God-qualities which you wish to cultivate and experience in everyday life. This truth is so important and astonishing that you may not grasp its full significance at first. *You already are!* As a son of God you automatically partake of His characteristics. You are part of That which created you. It is your heritage. The qualities of the Nature of God, the Father, constitute perfection, and you *are* born with them, you were created "in the image and likeness of God." If you were born of white American parents you do not have to seek Americanization nor strive to become a person of the white race; you just are. That is your inheritance. So, regardless of country or color, being a son of God you already possess God-like qualities.

It may take a good deal of thinking to get this settled in your consciousness, but when it is you will find that a big hurdle in your climb upward is overcome. It is a marvelous revelation to be able to grasp the significance of this magnificent truth — that you already possess the God-like qualities because they are your inheritance; God is what you are.

So far they may not have been showing forth in your life very clearly, but they are there. Much the larger portion of your quest is therefore completed upon this recognition. Your task now is to consciously bring these inner good qualities forth so that they can be expressed, used and experienced. Perhaps you may not have been very good at it previously. Perhaps you have had negative habits of thinking, feeling, and acting which kept blocking their right and full expression through you. If this is so, do not, at this time, concentrate your attention on what you want to get rid of. Instead, devote your efforts primarily to the development of the good qualities which you already possess, but which you have not been using.

## THINK OF YOUR GOAL;
## DISREGARD THE UNDESIRABLE

The quick and effectual way to eliminate anything you do not want is to disregard it and turn the attention and interest to what is directly opposite.

The first of the God-like qualities listed is Life. It may be that you have not been a very good example of the perfect Life of God. Possibly you have been ill or even right now think of yourself as in a run-down physical condition. If there is something you know you ought to be doing in an objective way to build up your health, of course do it. "God helps those who help themselves"; but your main work lies in your thinking. Instead of thinking illness or weakness, think life — Life!

Take time to think about what most fully represents exultant and joyous life — life that is so full of the sheer joy of living that it cannot be still! Young colts frisking in the pasture, kittens at play, children bubbling with energy! Think of them happily. Convince yourself and know that that Life fills your whole organism; that you not only *have* life but that you *are* Life! Dwell upon this thought, rejoice in it, declare it, give thanks for it, and accept Life as yours right now. Start expressing It in any and every way you can. Your life is the Life of God within you. Keep affirming this continuously. Accept your physical wholeness as the Perfection of God in you. Be happy about It and know that more and more It makes Itself manifest in your body.

## DO NOT BELITTLE YOUR DIVINE HERITAGE

Remember, you are God's creation; His Life is your life. Do not belittle that heritage!

It is possible that you need to cultivate the quality of Love more than any of the others. Recall the words of Jesus: "For one is your Father . . . and all ye are brethren." When you stop to really consider this truth, that God is your Father and that all others are your brothers, there cannot be any foundation for antagonism toward anyone, for God is not divided against Himself. This leaves the way open for loving thoughts about others and about yourself.

You are a child of God and therefore you should have a very high opinion of yourself. No foolish self-conceit, but a reverent understanding of your wondrous relationship to God. Tell yourself over and over again that the quality of Love lies within you and that it is only natural for you to be expressing It. Think first of those whom you love because of their nearness and dearness to you. Dwell upon their good qualities. Think of them by name and specify some admirable traits they possess. Kindle within your emotions a warm glow of feeling about them.

Now remember that all other people are just as truly worthy of your love, and are in need of it if they are to expand into finer and more beautiful ways of living. They need your love! Spend a few minutes with thoughts of love for all the world. It is sorely in need of every bit of help you can furnish, and love is its greatest need. This is not mere idle wishing. It is a definite service you can render. Your thoughts of love to mankind carry a blessing to mankind to the far corners of the globe. Do not neglect to exercise this privilege.

## YOU HAVE ACCESS TO THE WISDOM OF GOD

How you wish at times that you had a greater supply of wisdom-intelligence! But you already have it! Sit quietly by yourself and *know* that as God's child your wisdom is unlimited. Believingly, know that Universal Spirit, All-Wisdom, is now making known to you everything you need to know in order to make right decisions, correct choices, proper plans. You need to convince yourself, again and again, that infinite Wisdom is yours to use as you choose. Know that It responds immediately to your every demand. Believe it. Joyously accept it. Continue to assert this and your way will be made plain to you.

Do you feel that you are out of harmony with any person

or situation? Is there resentment in your thinking? Is there any
sign of jealousy or envy gnawing away inside you? Are you
fearful or worried about something? If any of these are disturb-
ing you, you need but turn your attention to the fact that God
can only be Peace and Harmony. Let go all the tenseness in
your body, forget all the mean feelings you may have, and let
the body, emotions, and mind rest in a deep awareness of that
Peace which is God. Be still, still, in every way, and accept that
Peace of God, knowing It now heals everything within you that
hurts and that Its calming action enfolds all your experience.
Think Peace, feel Peace. Know that you *are* Peace, because you
are a definite, specific expression of God manifesting as you.

## CREATIVITY IS AT THE CENTER OF YOU

As Life — Love, Wisdom, and Peace — functions through
your thinking there is nothing to hinder Its Creative Action in
and through you. The Father has given all power to you — the
son. When you recognize and express these qualities you have
always possessed, then you can use them creatively for a better
life. Beauty and Joy are two of Life's greatest attributes. Beauty
starts to shine through your life and to make Itself manifest because It flows from and is inherent in the other qualities. Life,
both inner and outer, becomes so enriched that Joy will permeate
your whole being. You experience all these qualities, not by
searching for them, but by recognizing them deep within yourself; they are your inheritance. Live these qualities, declare your
good, believe in it, and act accordingly. Then you achieve the
worth-while life.

You will not accomplish all this in one week; it is re-education of yourself, and that takes time, but you have made a
start. The results will encourage you to steadily continue. Others
will see a change in you much sooner than you will realize it
yourself. Do not analyze yourself too closely; just go ahead and
grow. Your acceptance and expression of the One Life will ever
expand.

By such simple procedures as these, men and women have been lifted out of unhappiness, illness, poverty, inharmony, and unemployment into wholesome, productive, and highly success-ful living. These are definite, scientific, and spiritual techniques. Follow them if you would achieve that glorious realm which awaits those who *choose to attain* and who act accordingly. *As He is so are we, in this world.*

# CHAPTER V

## YOU DETERMINE YOUR WELFARE

IN THE VERY BEGINNING of the Bible we find that man was given dominion over every living creature. To be sure, he did not become aware of this instantly. It has taken him eons to begin to realize it and start making it an actual fact. It is a statement of God's relationship to man and in Spirit it always has been true, just waiting for man's awareness of it. Again and again we find statements in the Old Testament beginning with the words, "I have given thee." It does eventually come to pass as an actual *fact*; but it has always been a *truth*. We need to keep clearly in mind the difference between a fact, something that is evident and concrete, and a truth, that which everlastingly *is*, whether we can see it or not.

It took man a long time to become aware of his dominion over all animals. Still more slow has been his conquest of conditions, but that is because he has been so involved in his conquest of himself. The old Greek advice, "Man, know thyself," is even yet of profound significance to us all. We need to more fully know ourselves if we are to lead the successful, happy, and useful life we desire. We see the necessity of knowing ourselves better, of understanding our spiritual nature. We must also know the relationship of our mind, body, and emotions so that we can control them wisely and direct them for our own welfare.

## THERE IS NO SEPARATION BETWEEN YOU AND GOD

All is Spirit. Spirit is Mind. Mind is One. There is no separation between God and you except to the degree you think you are separated. If you believe that you are locked in a room, and believe it so firmly that you do not even try the doors and windows, the results are exactly the same as though you were, though the actual truth may be that there is no lock and that you are free to go as you please. Your belief is all that lies between you and freedom. You need to forever banish the belief that there is any barrier between God and you. You are in God-Mind; you are of God-Mind; you *are* God-Mind made manifest in human form.

If you can get this settled in your mind you are ready for the next step: the conscious direction of thought so that right and good results are constantly being brought forth in your life. You want to be sure that your thinking is not in conflict with itself, and that there is clear, concise thought about your greatest good. You are also very much interested in experiencing right action in your body. If there is a way by which you can so use your thought as to create right conditions for you in your daily affairs, you certainly are interested in learning the way and applying it.

Science of Mind teaches you to so understand God's Law that you can live happily, successfully, with good health, and gradually grow in your expression of God within you. Whatever will tend toward these results should claim your attention. This is the kind of practical spiritual thinking you want.

## IMPROVE YOUR HABITS

Let us start with the subject of knowing yourself, and see if you can increase your acquaintance with a way of thought which you can use effectively, and with better results. We have found that infinite Mind, as Law, creates and sustains and is therefore of prime importance to us. The Law also maintains our persistent thought patterns as habits. Every day we should be adding to those habits which are desirable, now that we know how to do it, and how they work.

You can add to your supply of good habits by cultivating cheerfulness. It is one of the most helpful traits anyone can have. Thankfulness is another. When we Americans think of how much we have for which to be thankful, it would seem that every moment should be filled with gratitude. A happy expectancy of good is something to which more attention should be given until it becomes a fixed habit. You can think of many others, but unless you are really developing such habits you are not taking advantage of that exceedingly valuable aspect of the Law of Mind which is always ready and willing to accept whatever you insist upon, and sustain it as a habit which shall then function without your having to bother to think about it in particular.

## NOTHING IS FORGOTTEN

In this process of knowing yourself, however, you find that Mind in Its operation as Law — Its subjective nature — has another characteristic to which you must give attention. It is also the storehouse of memories of former experiences. Of course you have forgotten most of the trivial incidents of childhood, though some few remain vivid in your memory. Thousands of events, acts, circumstances, influences, and experiences of later life, also, whether or not you readily recall them, together with all those of childhood, are stored away in the subjective part of your mind. In very large measure they are what color your life today. Many of them have helped to form your attitudes of happiness, courage, self-reliance, hope, faith, initiative, industry, and all the other good qualities you have. Here also are stored the memories which may cause many of the negative experiences you encounter.

When we use the term "positive" we simply mean "good" qualities. When we speak of "negative" qualities we are using the word to mean those that are not good.

## YOUR TRUE NATURE IS THE NATURE OF GOD

No one is able to look back into his life and definitely determine just what it was which made such an impression upon him that he developed the positive qualities he now possesses.

Really, it is a sum total of particular impressions that makes up the main part of those influences enabling one to have the good qualities he now enjoys. The same is true in regard to the negative qualities. One really does not know how he came to have such attitudes, thought habits, or ways of reacting to certain conditions. Irritability, lack of poise, or any one of a dozen other negative character traits all seem to be a part of oneself. In many cases one does not even know that he has such characteristics.

"Why, that's just my nature; I've always been that way!" you may exclaim, if your attention is called to certain ways in which you are reacting to what affects you unpleasantly. And you are honest in saying this. But this isn't your *real* nature! No, you are made in the image and likeness of God. Therefore, in principle, you are perfect. You could not be otherwise because of your birthright.

What you *really* are is Life, Love, Wisdom, Peace, Power, Beauty, and Joy. These are your true characteristics. Anything different is something that has entered your thinking and has been placed in subjective mind where it is acted upon by the Law of Mind, whether you know it or not. Your thoughts, past and present, manifest in your conduct and relationship with others whom you contact.

"But if I don't know what is down there in my storehouse, what can I do about it?" you question, and it is only reasonable that you should. You first need to realize that there may be undesirable qualities in that storehouse of yours; and second, learn how to clean them out.

You no doubt can readily recall a number of incidents which you frankly admit left a scar on your thinking — something you don't forget, which continues to tinge your outlook. For each one that you do remember, however, there are probably dozens which have entirely faded from consciousness. Still, they are there, and steadily influencing or creating your total experience in life.

What to do about them? That's the question.

## GIVE THE LAW NEW INSTRUCTIONS

Remember that one very important trait of Mind in Its action as Law is obedience; It creates without question. It responds to your firm convictions and beliefs. This at once should settle any difficulty because now you know that your thought of good acting as a command and directive cleans out from that storehouse everything it contains which is negative and detrimental to your well-being. This does not mean that you must refresh your memory of old influences and events which did you harm. There is no need to know all about them, or review them, but you do want to get rid of them because you cannot afford to harbor any longer anything which is injurious.

When you make affirmative declarations, know perfectly well that they will be fulfilled; then keep your conscious thought free of doubts, or wondering as to *how* it should be done, or when. Otherwise you will be hindering the production of the desired results. It is a good thing to declare your good, the issuance of commands, when you are not thinking of a thousand other things. Only then will the Law of Mind have a clear and concise pattern for Its action. This is being explained in very simple language, but the process is profoundly important and one of the most valuable things you can learn.

There is no one without some negative ideas and concepts stored away in his subjective mind and he is probably totally unaware of many of them. Would it not then be wise for you to affirmatively declare every night, for as long as is necessary, that the highly important work of cleaning out the storehouse is now being done? Suppose you could banish the emotional rubbish that has been accumulating there for years and years in six months! Wouldn't that be about the most important thing you could do?

## ELIMINATE THE OBJECTIONABLE HABIT

All during the day, and as you are about to fall asleep, think of all the positive and desirable character traits you can, whether you are now expressing them or not. Then declare that all that is contrary to them is cleared out, and that only the positive, desirable, and good traits are being established as your experience by the creative action of your thought. *Know* that they fill your whole life and being. Be confident and happy in the knowledge that it is entirely within your right, power, and ability to discard and remove the wrong thought patterns of the past. Get a thorough job of cleaning done, and you immediately start to fill your whole experience with what is God-like.

Continuously, day and night, this willing, powerful, obedient servant, the Law of Mind, is busy fulfilling your orders — your *believing* thought. It will not be long until you can begin to see the difference in yourself; others will see it much sooner. Your whole mental and emotional attitude will change. You will become a new person, completely made over by the Creative Action of God within you.

## YOU ARE NEVER A FAILURE UNTIL YOU ADMIT IT

Some old negative patterns of thought have resulted in frustrations. They have made you feel that, at least in regard to some of your great desires, you are a failure. You may have been balked in every endeavor along certain lines. There may have been a tendency to become bitter in regard to such matters. Now all this is gone! You now know that all things are possible. Perhaps you see that the very disappointments you met forced you into something better, or that you can now use them as steppingstones to greater results.

Perhaps some of the experiences of the past had hurt you cruelly; your emotional nature felt a deep, deep injury and you would never forget that event! Well, it doesn't matter whether you have forgotten it or not. It is now healed and rendered ineffective for you have insisted, declared, and demanded and accepted that all negatives be cleared away; the obedient, willing, powerful Action of God-Mind within you has done it. Although you may feel you have been talking to yourself, remember that *all mind is one,* and you really have been committing this matter to the Action of Universal Mind. That is why the results are so sure and so eminently satisfactory.

## INFERIORITY IS NO PART OF GOD'S MAN

You may never have admitted that you were inferior to others, but there probably have been times when you felt timid, shy, inadequate, or fearful about attempting something. These are evidences of a thought pattern deep within you which silently suggested that you were inferior, and you accepted that suggestion even if you didn't put it into words. Let's give this matter a little more attention.

We are trying to follow the old Greek adage: "Man, know thyself." Truly to know yourself is to realize deeply, sincerely, and constantly that you are made in the image and likeness of God. Therefore, all God-like qualities are inherent in you. How, then, could you be inferior to anyone? It would be impossible! You not only have but you *are* Life, Love, Wisdom, Peace, Power, Beauty, and Joy. If any previous ideas have made you feel otherwise, know that whatever they are, they are *now* being cleansed away and that from now on you are asserting your dominion over any negative thinking that would seem to keep you from your greater good. Reason it out and come to know that there is absolutely nothing that can deny God in you. Your conscious mind, however, must back itself up by the complete cooperation of your every thought — the continual implanting of affirmative ideas of good. This is how you are putting the Law to work in the right way every day and every night.

## EMPHASIZE LOVE AND RIGHTEOUSNESS

You cannot afford to live with a feeling of inferiority — you are God's son! Automatically you get rid of the negatives by the implanting of positives. Negatives cannot exist when positives fill the space. When the sunshine of love and confidence fills your whole being, the darkness of the negatives has to disappear. The attitudes of your emotional nature — the feeling level — are what decide your conduct. The heart is the symbol of the deepest emotions, so whatever you are at heart, whether you recognize it or not, is the key to what you really are. "For as [a man] thinketh in his heart, so is he" is a scientific law; use it daily. Reconstruction has to begin in your heart — your feeling nature. This is why a cleansing of negative past habits and memories is of primary importance. There needs to be a re-education of emotional reactions.

One of the first requisites for a happy and successful life is good health. You cannot be healthy if you harbor *enemies* of wholeness: resentment, fear, self-centeredness, and feelings of guilt. Psychologists and physicians say these are the four great enemies of human personality. To banish them you do not pin your attention on them; instead, you emphasize their opposites, those characteristics which Jesus urged: Love, Faith, Unselfishness, and Moral Rightness.

W. P. Newsholme, in *Health, Disease and Integration,* says: "Hate is poison, not only moral and spiritual poison, but mental and physical poison, as well."

Dr. E. Stanley Jones cites the following incident:

"At the close of a meeting, a lady came to me, and in a frightened voice said, 'Well, if anger may produce a stomach ulcer, I'm never going to get angry again!'

"She wouldn't listen when 'Thou shalt not hate' was written in the Bible, but she sat up and took notice when she found it was written also in her own stomach."

From the very first there has been advocated the wisdom and necessity of simple ideas and rules which will help you use the principles of Science of Mind for peace of mind, health of body, and success in every phase of living.

Always there is the need of following them happily. This is because the three aspects of man's nature are so closely interrelated that what affects one part has a very definite bearing on all other parts of his nature. You can build bodily health by being emotionally healthy, happy, enthusiastic, hopeful. As you stimulate concepts of spiritual wholeness you intensify joyous emotional activity.

Your efforts are to increase your awareness of spiritual power. The start was with the body, because you are a little better acquainted with it, and see the necessity of accepting the stimulus of spiritual power in and through it. Know that the good cheer, the happiness, the joyous expectancy that you are building up in consciousness is being reflected in your health, your financial success, and in your ability to live a fuller and more abundant life. *Man determines his own welfare.*

# CHAPTER VI

## THE POWER OF DIRECTED EMOTIONS

THE SPECIAL ATTRIBUTE of self-consciousness is that which gives us the power of choice. This is certainly a supreme gift of God to man. It enables him to choose his own destiny — accepting Divine Wisdom and Power in such ways that he can have that chosen destiny become his experience.

It is, however, an outstanding truth that every privilege brings its corresponding responsibility. The right and power to make your own decisions, bad or good, puts you in a very vital position. You now realize you are no longer an automaton, moved about by the caprice of circumstance, solely guided by instincts, or subject to some will superimposed upon you. You are free to choose! But you have to take the consequences of that choosing. You shall have, and do have, whatever you recognize and accept as yours. *All things await man's recognition and acceptance!*

The universal creative Law of Mind, of which you are a part, creates for you according to your choice. Too often that choice is determined by emotional attitudes, without due regard to thoughtful decision. Too often it is a negative emotional re-action which directs your decisions rathers than the process of logical thinking — that ability of the conscious mind which enables you to think things out clearly and decide accordingly.

### EVERYTHING ACCORDING TO LAW

What you are deeply *feeling* is usually what you are establishing in Mind as cause; it is the pattern for what you will receive.

To make this more clear, even though you may have thought of it before, think about the soil in the garden. When you wish to produce a crop of any kind you first prepare the soil, using your best knowledge to get it into the right condition so it will bring forth what you want to grow there. When the earth is well prepared, free from obstructions, properly fertilized, and in every way made ready to receive the seed; when the rain and the sun have done their part and you have carefully selected your seeds and made your plans, then you begin the planting. You plant *only* those seeds that will grow into what you want in your garden. You may want a row of radishes in between one of beets and one of carrots. Close by, in the same soil, you plant cabbages, and then next, perhaps, watermelons.

From the good, reliable, dependable soil the radish seed draws whatever is needed to produce white radishes with red skins. But, from exactly the same soil, in the very next row, you get carrots, bright orange-yellow all the way through and tasting not one bit like the radishes, and on the other side are deep red beets of still another texture and taste. All the other kinds of seeds bring forth according to their own natures, and — *this is the point* — you knew they would! That is why you planted them. No one is wise enough to pick out of the soil the chemicals to produce the different results, but then no one has to. Your part is fourfold: Get the soil ready; choose the right seeds; plant them; and give the garden the right care and attention. The marvelously wise soil of Mother Nature takes charge of the processes of production.

No one can explain how or why this happens. But then, just because of lack of such understanding, do we fail to take advantage of it? No. Year after year, millions of men and women plant their gardens and know in advance what harvest they are going to have.

In the spiritual realm, Universal Subjective Mind as Law is the soil. It is just as dependable, just as reliable, and functions just as naturally as the soil in the garden. It takes whatever you choose to plant in It, and It produces accordingly. You, personally, are the one who determines what kind of results you are going to have. That is one of the principles you need to keep constantly in mind. That which you decide with the conscious mind and then commit to the action of the Law, in quiet trust, in perfect confidence, is that which will come to pass for you. No one knows just how thoughts become concrete and tangible. Neither does anyone know how one part of the soil produces a carrot when the very same soil, only a few inches away, brings forth a luscious watermelon. But just because the action is not completely understood, has this kept one from planting seeds? You need to be equally wise and trustful about your spiritual planting.

## CAREFUL PREPARATION

Care was used in preparing the garden soil in order to get it into the proper condition. Here again the analogy is true: We must remove from the creative medium of mind all negatives. It must be at peace. It has to have removed from it everything that would obstruct the right development of the good results sought. When you are poised, calm, at peace, filled with happy expectancy, serenely trusting in the fulfillment of the highest good, you are ready to do your spiritual planting.

All summer long the warmth of the sun and the refreshment of gentle rains bring your garden through the various stages of growth to rich maturity, the reason you planted it. Your spiritual garden, first planted in the soil of emotional serenity, you keep nourished with love and watered with expectancy. Do not let any weeds of doubt or anxiety hinder its progress. Give it daily attention, entirely free from worry or fear as to the outcome. Remember, you can trust the soil to do its part if you but do your part!

## CAREFUL PLANTING

If there had been no soil you could have had no garden. Further, the soil had to be in the right condition. So it is with your spiritual garden. You are always planting something —

desires, longings, and hopes, or fears and worries. There is no special season set aside for this kind of planting. Therefore, the subjective-mind soil must be in the right condition all the time. You are always planting and you cannot afford to have the good seeds dropped into soil which contains a mass of weeds. You cannot afford to be planting bad seeds — thoughts of negation, worries, fears, angers, hates, resentments. Such seeds will grow just as rapidly as the good seeds and will bring forth a crop just as sure and abundant. The soil of the garden has no power nor inclination to reject bad seeds while accepting good ones. Your subjective-mind level, the creative medium of Law, also is entirely impersonal and will just as readily take your negations and produce a crop of illness, poverty, hardship, difficulty, or inharmony. Be careful about your planting!

When you first start to get your garden ready you are likely to find that it contains a good many stones, weeds, hard chunks of earth, or rubbish. These need to be cleaned away if the soil is to produce as you desire. Similarly, old complexes, attitudes, and habits certainly will ruin your harvest in the spiritual realm unless you get them out.

One thing, often, that has to be removed is a sense of inferiority. All that is really needed to get rid of it is to truly realize that you are God's child, God is what you are. As such you are inferior to no one! Some may be more talented along certain lines than you, but deep within each lies the very same Life, expressing in each in an individual manner — each has his particular talents and abilities. You are made in the image and likeness of God, and therefore you *cannot* be inferior to anyone in the world!

A superiority complex is also a type of weed no one wants flourishing in his garden. It is removed by again realizing that all are God's children and filled with His qualities; that each is a superior expression of Life and expresses that Life according to his nature.

To bring about continuous unfoldment and the accomplishment of desired results, get your emotional garden cleaned up. Then do the right kind of planting.

## FORGIVE YOURSELF

Even though you may not be troubled by what are usually known as inferiority or superiority complexes, still you may have a sense of self-condemnation which thwarts your efforts toward happiness and success and keeps you so disturbed that your highest efficiency is impaired. To be out of harmony with oneself is, indeed, a sad condition. In speaking of self-condemnation we mean that frame of mind which a generation ago would have been referred to as a guilty conscience.

Many were brought up to be so deeply aware of some sort of a critical inner monitor, which was usually accusing us of something, that it is pretty hard to get away from it. The sad part of it is that with a more mature judgment many have come to know that most of the little things which were considered "wicked" in childhood are now found to have nothing of evil in them. Early training may have led some to a belief that the wearing of bright colors, for instance, was a sin. To read a story, no matter how high the moral tone, if it were not an actual fact, was evil. These and a hundred other narrow restrictions bind and limit people. Because you were just an ordinary boy or girl, with a natural yearning for what was banned, you found some way to avail yourself of the forbidden color, or you secretly and guiltily read the book.

Ever since then you may have been burdened with a sense of having committed a sin. Such self-condemnation hangs over one as a cloud, obscuring the outgiving of God's Love and the expression of His Nature. All should live a full, free, and abundant life. These illustrations may seem very insignificant, but they are indicative of the sources of many a troubled mind. Even though they may not be active in the conscious mind, they remain active at the subjective level, coloring attitudes and actions.

## A FALSE SENSE OF GUILT

A true story is told of a young woman in a very religious family whose brother was a military officer. On the occasion of a visit to the city by the, then, Prince of Wales, this young officer was chosen as one of the bodyguards at a celebration given in honor of the Prince. Proud of the beauty of his lovely sister and eager to have her share his temporary honor, he insisted that she be his partner as they led the grand march at the beginning of the festivities. She consented and had the thrill of her lifetime. Later, however, she realized that she had — at least, almost — joined in a dance, something her family considered wicked and worldly. She grieved over this, feeling that with her upbringing it was entirely inexcusable. No doubt much of this condemnation was the criticism, either spoken or unspoken, on the part of others whose opinions she respected.

We need to be thankful that an All-wise Father has planted within us a guide to right conduct which we call conscience! But also how careful we need to be that we do not allow it to destroy our happiness because of something which, when seen with correct judgment, we can realize has no moral wrong. Dr. Smiley Blanton tells us that "unless the growth of conscience is wisely directed the results will be serious conflict." He adds: "In the process of conscience-building there are four phases:

1. A primitive impulse of love.
2. A profound need for holding our parents' love and being obedient to them.
3. A synthesis of the child's impulse for self-criticism with the parental criticism.
4. The modification of all these feelings by the contact with life."

Three of these phases of development take place in child-hood. Then through all the mature years much time is spent trying to get rid of that which had been fostered in the early formative years of conscience. The sad part of it is that a lot of the harm done is never undone. One may outgrow the feeling that parents are watching and blaming one for shortcomings, but one is likely to transfer the same feeling to a deep conviction that God is watching for every misdoing, is blaming one, and that certain punishment of some kind is being handed out, or stored up. Often this goads one on to doing other and much worse "sins." Certainly, when one has done wrong one ought to be sorry about it, and promptly mend his ways. But to be wallowing in negative emotions, and not doing anything constructive about the matter will do no good.

The complexes — bad weeds — have to be rooted out of your spiritual garden. And the way to remove a negative is to turn the attention to its opposite, positive good, and cultivate it.

We know the qualities of God's Nature and we know how to develop them. The conscious mind must learn to sit in the driver's seat and direct what is to take place. Emotions can be controlled; and if you are to be a successful gardener you must see to it that the right kind of planting is done. You must learn to rule your own life! " . . . he that ruleth his spirit [is better] than he that taketh a city."

If you are to be in control of your life you shall have to assert control over your emotions and keep them under the guidance of your clear thinking, which can be Divinely guided and inspired.

Even the simplest little device which brings this procedure down from the abstract and puts it into concrete form is exceedingly helpful. Any expedient which tends to make you *feel* that you are taking the right step will be of tangible value.

Learn to praise yourself for the qualities you want to develop. Be as kind and encouraging to yourself as you would be to anyone else trying to improve. Your whole life — thought, body, and emotions — will soon respond to the praise you give it and you will really develop the good qualities desired! Remember, you are always planting something!

# CHAPTER VII

## THE "PERSONALITY" OF VALUE

WHATEVER EFFORTS ARE NECESSARY to develop a good personality will bring adequate and satisfying returns. The time will be well spent, the efforts well rewarded.

If there is a type of personality that pays — and there is — you naturally desire to know more about it so that you may bring it forth in your own life and be in a position to reap the benefits from it. First of all, what is personality? For many years philosophers and psychologists have discussed this elusive something known as personality; and they have tried to explain it, they have sought to show its desirability and how to acquire it. Probably they will continue to do so, and the longer they do the greater will be the number of definitions given.

A definition which seems to meet our requirements at this time is: *Personality is the way a man expresses his individuality.* Let us separate it into its key parts and see if we can reveal its true significance.

"Personality . . ." is comprised of the characteristics one displays, the degree to which he has developed certain traits and qualities, and the way in which he shows them forth in his life — appearance, speech, actions, attitudes, the way he appears to the rest of the world.

". . . expresses his individuality." Personality is the result of what one does — his thinking, his emotions, his actions — with what he *thinks* he is, his individuality. He is the son of God, individualizing all the qualities of God. According to this spiritual heritage, he has every characteristic of his Father: Life, Love, Wisdom, Peace, Power, Beauty, and Joy.

## WHAT YOU THINK YOU ARE PROCLAIMS ITSELF

The more you come to realize your true spiritual nature the more you will be able to let it flow through you and express as your personality; the more you will be able to show to all the world your understanding of Life. The clearer your thoughts are about your real nature the more you will be able to experience it, and both you and all those about you will benefit. You are an individual and must express that individuality to the fullest extent as your personality. But you must always remember your Source — God's Nature.

To the extent that you fail to recognize or express your individuality, to that degree you will be denying yourself the experience of the joyous attributes of Life — God. That which others know you to be through your personality will be good or bad depending upon what you know you are. So proclaim yourself in no uncertain terms, in the highest terms and qualities that you know God to be.

## PERSONALITY ADVANTAGES

Now that you know the possibility of developing a good personality, let us consider some of its aspects.

*Social.* This is probably of greater importance than any other trait one may possess. Those with a good social personality get along well with others; they are always desirable associates. The simple, easy, but sure way to test your own personality in this respect is to ask yourself candidly, "Do people like to have me around?" If they do, you may be sure that your social personality is a pleasing one. Of what value to you is it to have them like to have you around? Well, it practically insures your holding your position. It brings you opportunities for advancement and it draws to you many friends. It is pleasing and gratifying to have a large number of friends; often it is the secret of progress, abundance, and fine opportunities for increased useful self-expression. It makes life an eminently happy experience. It does pay to have people like to have you around.

*Physical.* A good personality asset is good physical health. Health of body is the outpicturing of health of mind. If you accept the Perfection of God indwelling you, you automatically assure yourself of good health. If there were no other inducement to the cultivation of a good personality, this in itself would be enough.

*Financial.* The rewards of a God-like personality are beyond computation. It holds the secret to abundance. It insures business and professional success and opens the way for financial remuneration. Often financial rewards rest to a considerable extent on one's ability to bring all his capabilities to bear on a situation. One whose personality is agreeable, kindly, considerate, and tolerant usually meets little or no opposition. He does not have to fight for what he knows is right. In fact, others easily fall in line with what is good and right. If, temporarily, he finds it necessary to set aside his own desires, he does it gracefully and in a short time events and conditions become readjusted and he soon finds things going in the right way. Personality is the root of one's financial success when he expresses what he *is*.

*Spiritual.* The individual who attunes himself to God accomplishes much in his personality development, the expression of his individuality. He is constantly striving to reproduce in his own life high spiritual qualities, and as a result they are daily becoming more and more fully expressed. He is so deeply interested in being about the "Father's business" that he steadily grows in his ability to reflect the attributes of God.

One with a well-developed personality is of course a happy person. As the result of social, physical, financial, and spiritual well-being, happiness is assured. Even in the midst of the varied requirements of a busy life he is ever serene, poised, and at peace with himself, his fellow men, and his God.

## THE PERSONALITY THAT PAYS

We arrive, then, at three conclusions concerning the type of personality that pays.

1. A good personality is the sending forth of those God-qualities which lie inherent in you.
2. It enables you to live so that your presence is desired — others "like to have you around."
3. This results in having better advantages in many ways than would otherwise be possible. One of these is the opportunity to experience more abundance, including money.

Here are some interesting illustrations.

During the worst years of the depression, a group of psychologists from Harvard set out to investigate for themselves the real cause for many of the dismissals from employment which were so prevalent. They knew that business was exceedingly dull and did not warrant keeping the full quota of men, but why were some discharged and others retained? What was the determining factor? If this could be decided it might be of great help to many and enable them to avoid discharge. With work so curtailed and re-employment difficult to attain, it would be a very valuable bit of information.

The investigation involved the cases of 4,000 men in Boston for a period of a year, and represented all classes of workers — unskilled, skilled, professional, clerical, and executive, so as to get a general cross section of the situation.

In every case the actual facts were secured from both sides — employer and employee.

Here are some of the startling facts that were revealed:

The reports showed that instead of the majority of dismissal reasons being "poor business," "necessity for curtailing," "reducing overhead," and similar remarks, which the investigators expected to receive, they found that only a small number of those who had been dismissed had lost their jobs because of such reasons. When all the figures were compiled, it was found that:

16% had lost their jobs because of inefficiency or distinct lack of ability in their particular work.

8% were out of work because of immorality — in a few cases gross misdemeanors.

13% had been dismissed for miscellaneous reasons, including the decrease of business of the firm.

63% made up the remainder and all of them had lost their positions in that crucial period, when it was practically impossible to get other employment, simply because they did not get along well with their associates!

The survey showed that in one year, in one city, out of 4,000 cases investigated, a total of 2,520 men were out of a chance to make a living, not because of not being needed, not for any crime, not because of lack of ability, but simply because their personalities were such that others did not "like to have them around"!

If no other illustrations were ever encountered, this survey should be enough to prove the money value of a pleasing personality.

## PERSONALITY QUOTIENT

During the past twenty or thirty years business and professional men, and especially educators, have been paying much attention to the individual's "Intelligence Quotient." "How high is his I.Q.?" is often one of the first questions asked in regard to one being considered for almost any position. This is done often to insure that workers are placed for their greatest benefit. However, any good thing can be carried too far; any virtue may become a vice by overemphasis. This may be the case in regard to the I.Q. In the last few years keen, hard-headed business employers have come to see that a man's I.Q. is not nearly so important as is his P.Q. (Personality Quotient), and this is what they are now insisting upon. "Is he the kind of person who makes friends easily, gets along well with the public, as well as with his co-workers? Will he be an asset to the firm?"

With this in view, authorities at one of our leading universities decided to make a survey as to the relative merits of the I.Q. and the P.Q. in the experiences of some of their graduates. At Commencement Day, one year, a group of 100 brilliant I.Q. men were listed, without their knowing it, and their careers watched for results. All of them had done remarkably well academically, but had failed to mix with their fellows, probably because of their great interest in studies. They had been the typical introvert type, interested solely in meeting high educational standards and consequently shutting themselves off from their companions.

Another group of 100, chosen the same day from the graduating class, consisted of men whose academic standings had been so mediocre that they had only barely succeeded in passing, but whose genial qualities of personality had made them so popular that they were greatly liked by all who knew them. They had probably given of themselves in student activities too freely for the good of their own scholastic records, but all through their college careers they had had happy and useful associations and had made many friends.

In neither of the two groups did anyone know he was being made the subject of a test.

## THE PROOF OF THE PUDDING

Because of the fact that it usually takes a professional man from five to seven years to get established, as he passes through the so-called "starvation period," the university authorities felt it would not be fair to announce any results until all had had ten years in which to prove themselves. This, they felt, would be a reasonable test, and they were eager to see what they could learn as to the relative values of the much-vaunted high I.Q. as against the low I.Q. but high P.Q.

The group of 100 was large enough to average out individual

exceptions. It really constituted a good test. At the end of the ten years it was found that the brilliant I.Q. men on the average were making $3,000 a year. The P.Q. men were averaging $10,000!

These men liked people; people liked them, liked to have them around. They progressed in their business or profession, led happy lives, and made money.

To develop a personality that pays — pays in good dollars and cents, in happiness, friendships, and health — is something of specific interest to all of you. It is a definite part of your spiritual training. It is one of the steps in that upward climb which takes us into greater spiritual awareness. Such aspiration has its rightful place for it points the way to wholesome, happy, efficient, God-like living. How shall we attain such a personality — one that pays?

## THE HIGH PRIVILEGE OF RIGHT THINKING

We need to constantly remind ourselves of the God-like qualities which lie within us by nature, and renew our daily persistent efforts to bring them up into manifestation in our lives. We now see even more reasons why we should be cultivating them. It is a process of thought and spiritual awareness, but it does need constantly to be accompanied by those objective activities which translate all our high resolves and rich aspirations into action. In your contact with everyone you must be aware of the necessity and the high privilege of putting all the good, kindly, thoughtful, helpful, encouraging, and inspiring qualities into actual practice as you deal with people.

Your thoughts must be right, your motives right, your eagerness to build God-like lives far more outstanding than a desire to be a good money-maker. "Seek ye first the kingdom of God, and his righteousness, and all these things shall be added unto you," is a statement one cannot afford to ignore.

Your thinking must be right, and remember what is said in Philippians: "Whatsoever things are true . . . honest . . . just . . .

pure . . . lovely . . . of good report; if there be any virtue, and if there be any praise, think on these things." This is not only good moral advice, but it is psychologically sound, and it is good common sense.

You have seen the reasons why you ought to be cultivating a fine personality; you have seen the advantages of it, common sense tells you to do it. It is your privilege, and responsibility, to cultivate the "personality that pays." *Be ye transformed by the renewing of your mind.*

## SOME THINGS TO REMEMBER

If there is anything you dislike about your work or environment, state clearly in one sentence what it is you do want. For example, you might be saying, "My work is dull and monotonous, and I do not like my associates." Now change that thought to one which expresses exactly the opposite: "I am steadily finding new interest in my work and pleasing qualities in those about me." Regardless of what your problem is, do your best to affirm its opposite, that which you want, all day and evening. You may not succeed so well the first day, or week, but keep it up for a whole month and see if you do not completely rebuild your attitude in regard to that certain problem. This practice will pay rich rewards.

Make a practice of looking for the good in others and praising them for it. Make yourself do this!

Think of the qualities you may particularly need in your own special work — alertness, energy, initiative, speed, appearance, faithfulness, poise, or cheerfulness. Whatever it is, resolve to improve yourself. You are the only one who can improve your personality, but it is so important, and anything which helps you do it is valuable to you. *Be ye transformed by the renewing of your mind*, and you and your affairs will be renewed as you transform your thinking.

# CHAPTER VIII

## FINDING LIFE'S RICHES

WHAT MAN BELIEVES AND DOES determine the results he gets! But some may say, "That may be very good theory but it doesn't work out in actual life. I've always done the best I could but things don't go right for me. I'm not one of the lucky ones!"

### YOU ALONE CHOOSE YOUR GOOD

We are once again impressed with the fact that the responsibility for what one experiences is thrown back upon him. This is but the direct result of being human, of possessing consciousness — that degree of development which gives man his right and power of choice. Because we live in a democracy we are particularly insistent upon our right to do as we choose in our affairs. In the realm of Spirit we should be equally appreciative of such a privilege.

The primary fact is that we desire greater good — health, money, harmony, better business, greater supply, different and better employment, or anything else which will add to our joy of living. How does Science of Mind teach us to get it?

It is only common sense to say that first of all you need to understand spiritual Law — that Law which you are attempting to use. You need to remind yourself that Spirit surrounds you and is unlimited, and is the Source of all things; also that It is always becoming something in your experience, and that something is decided by you. You must remember that Law is entirely impartial and neutral. It does not care what demand is made upon It. It produces whatever is planted in It, just as does the soil in a garden. Certainly by this time you do have that understanding. You know about this spiritual activity even if you do not always use it for your good.

Even though the illustration is very simple and though it has already been given repeatedly, remember that you cannot understand the processes which are carried on in your garden as the various seeds develop into plants. You do not, however, wait for a complete understanding of this marvelous process of nature; you just go ahead and make use of it. This is your guide for right now. What does it matter if you do not see how a thing you desire can be? It is results you are after; that's what counts!

## ACCEPT AND USE GOD'S LAW

You know that the radish seed will produce radishes and *nothing else*; and you know that the *only thing* that can grow from your carrot seed will be carrots. Because you *know*, you act accordingly. You *accept* this as a law of nature on which you can depend. Let's see now if you cannot be just as sensible in the matter of your spiritual planting. It is that same kind of acceptance which you need with respect to the use of the spiritual planting process. Such acceptance has to be a deep conviction, a perfect belief. Do not try by force of will to compel yourself into this belief. Let go all striving — God's way of doing things must be the best way. Wouldn't it be wise and easy just to say to yourself, "This is the way such things are done. I have learned enough to know that this is God's method of getting results and I accept it. I believe it. I know it is so! Yes, I accept.

"The particular result to which I am now giving my attention is already mine. The great limitless Source of supply is merely waiting for me to place my order. Because I have grasped sufficient understanding of infinite Law to know that this is the way my good comes to me, and because I have chosen what it shall be, I am meeting the requirements of the Law, and so I *know* this particular good is mine, *now*.

"I *feel* the experience of it. I picture myself enjoying it. I see its desirability and value. I am planning how it adds to my experience of worthy living. Because of what it is to me, or the

special ways in which I use this good, I am of greater helpfulness and inspiration to others. This is one of the reasons why I
chose it. I know that my main work in life is to 'be about my
Father's business,' and this good makes me able to do that more
effectively. Whatever I receive is only being entrusted to me as
a worthy steward of God's abundance.

"It is only as I use talents, privileges, opportunities, respon-
sibilities, or funds wisely that they shall be of benefit to me. I
shall not bury them in the ground, I shall not hoard them; I shall
*use* them constantly so that they shall serve others and in that
service shall increase. I shall produce intelligently and plentifully
with what is entrusted to me. The good I have chosen is now
mine!"

## FAITH UNIFIED WITH WORKS

This is the process of building a Mental Equivalent. You
need to actually feel that the desired good is yours *now*! And it
will be! This is the Law; It manifests what we accept. *This is
Faith.*

When this deep consciousness has been reached, it is well
to put the specific desire into words and to speak them forth with
perfect assurance of your right and power to do so. This plants
the seed in the spiritual soil, and it so confirms the result in your
own consciousness that you feel a rich and happy satisfaction
in knowing that you have now done your part in the creative
sequence. You have prepared the soil, chosen your seed, and
planted it. It is now committed to the Creativity of infinite Spirit
— Law — which brings forth your crop.

The declaration is the step in the process which unifies Faith
with Works. It is the affirmative thought made with spiritual
awareness, with understanding and acceptance. On the other
hand, if you had not made your declaration the procedure would
have lacked the necessary tie-up between Faith and Works.

The fundamental thing you have to remember is that this

is a spiritual process of making yourself fully receptive; so with an attitude of perfect acceptance make your declaration.

Your mental garden, however, will not be a success unless you tend it. It's going to be real work to make it produce the desired results, but you will not be satisfied with anything less than complete fulfillment.

## THE JOY OF RIGHT ACTION

From the Mental Equivalent part of our endeavor we now move to the Right Action part. There is work to be done. To be sure, the first part is of prime importance, for unless you had chosen your good and declared it there would have been nothing from which to expect returns. Still, if .you do not give it continuous attention you need not expect much of a return. It's going to demand your affirmative thinking all the time. But you will be so thrilled by what you see developing and by the satisfaction that always comes from achievement that it will not seem difficult. In fact, it is really a pleasure and you are richly repaid for all you do. The good you have chosen and planted in the realm of Cause requires definite action on your part, and it needs to be Right Action too!

"God does *for* us what He does *through* us" is a truth of such importance that you can never afford to ignore it. "God helps those who help themselves" is but another way of putting it.

Everything you can do objectively to promote this chosen good is, of course, what you are going to be doing. Anything less would be childish and infantile. You don't expect to get anything without paying the right price for it. That price, in the objective world, usually consists of good work, systematic study, personal development, or any concrete action that represents your part in the transaction. Nobody should ever want to get something for nothing. When you planted your garden you knew it would require tending all summer. Now you have planted some great, sincere, worthy desire in the realm of Cause and you are just as sincerely willing and eager to do your objective part in order that it shall be developed for you. This is Right Action. This is *Works*. Now *faith without works is dead*.

## DECLARE RIGHT ACTION INTO OPERATION

The expression Right Action also has a still deeper and slightly different meaning. During your meditation time, when you know what your choice is, when you know that it is a worthy one, and particularly when you know that it is secondary to the basic one, "Seek ye first the kingdom of God," you also know that, in most cases, the concrete development of it will involve activity on the part of other people. It may be that some one needs to participate in a certain way, it may include the cooperation of several persons, or a readjustment of a situation that now seems to stand in the way of the fulfillment of your good desire. Whatever it is, no one is wise enough to know just what and how everything should take place.

You need always to remember that even when you understand a situation thoroughly, and use your very best judgment, when you think you can clearly see conditions, circumstances, and results, still finite mind — your individual mind — can see only superficially. Infinite Mind can see and know all that is underneath, above, and around, past, present, and future, all of which is entirely shut off from your limited vision. The particular adjustment which you may think is desirable, may not, after all, be the right one. There may be a dozen different aspects of which you know nothing, and all of them may have a definite bearing on the right outcome of this desired good of yours. What, then, can you do? Will you throw up your hands in helpless despair, saying, "What's the use? I don't know what ought to be"?

Not at all! Man's mind is a particular expression of God-Mind through which God's Wisdom, as a creative and directive action, may be brought to bear upon particular situations and circumstances. Such action is always right, because it is God-Action. Therefore, part of your declaration is setting into motion whatever shall be "Right Action" in order that what is best for all shall be brought to pass. With perfect assurance you may declare this Right Action as taking place. Then you are sure of the right results.

## DO NOT OUTLINE

Some of your most carefully thought out and diligently carried out physical activities may seem for the time being to fail in promoting your desired good. Do not judge too quickly. It may be just a step toward the fulfillment of those unseen processes which are being carried on, which eventually will bring to pass what is wanted. No hasty judgment should be made as to the effectiveness or noneffectiveness of what you have done. Back of it all there must be a calm assurance that "Right Action" is manifesting in the events that occur, for you believingly and specifically have declared your acceptance of It. Whether that Right Action be in your own efforts, the work of others, or any one of a hundred different events, contacts, influences, or circumstances, it does not matter. You can be certain that what is right is being done.

It is a definite process extending through the steps of intellectual understanding of spiritual Law, emotional conviction that the chosen good is truly yours, the oral declaration of it to fasten it firmly in your consciousness, and the final knowledge that it is established as the law of your experience. There is also spiritual realization that everything shall conform to law and order, and that nothing, nothing, can keep your good from being developed in the right way and delivered to you. There always must be the physical activity on your part which shall round out the complete procedure. This is the combination of Faith and Works which guarantees success.

## NORMAL GROWTH

About a week or so after you had planted your garden, did you come home one afternoon to spend an hour or two working in it? Did you look it over and decide it was a failure because it had not come to maturity? Did you decide that it was all a mistake on your part to think that you were going to reap any results? Did you say, "Nothing came of it. I'll never try that again"? Certainly you did not. You knew it would take time. It takes time for one to grow in spiritual knowledge and realize the power of declaration, acceptance, and activity. Growth is not instantaneous; it is gradual. Results do not often come immediately. In nearly all cases, the desired results come to pass through normal human agencies. If we need more money, it does not rain down from the sky. It comes to us through natural, normal channels. In practically all cases the fulfillment of your desires is tied up with other people and what they think, say, and do. The Right Action you have decreed may prove to be something that involves considerable time. But you have to accept, right now, that the desired results are manifest.

When you know deep in your heart that what is right is taking place, even though you see no evidence of progress, you surely have no occasion for impatience or disappointment. Happily, expectantly, you go ahead doing what seems wise, energetically and enthusiastically, but free from all stress or strain. Your order has been placed in the Universal Storehouse, and there is nothing to be concerned about.

Remember these two points:

1. Your own spiritual awareness is growing.
2. The events, influences, and activities to produce Right Action for you are going through the natural process which is to bring the right result, whether or not you see the steps in the process.

If you had had no experience in the planting, cultivating, and tending of crops it would be foolish to start with a thousand-acre farm of diversified products. It would be better to begin with a few acres while you were learning farming principles. Gradually you would get ready for larger ventures later on with increased assurance and fewer doubts. The same is true in the spiritual realm. It is wise to use this principle in the little affairs of everyday living. To become skillful you may need to practice much. The principle is unfailing but you need skill in using it. Don't postpone the positive use of the Law for good until faced with a big emergency. Practice today on the small needs. Surely there isn't a day without its own special requirements, small, perhaps, but confronting you *now* and demanding solution. Begin today taking all your hour-by-hour needs and applying to them the principle of Faith and Works. Just such simple matters as these may present themselves:

I want to get that little matter of the neighborhood squabble of the children adjusted.

I need to make better collections of my bills this month.

My place of business needs some better arrangements and equipment.

How shall I make my advertising bring better results?

Greater harmony in my family and among my workers ought to be brought about.

I need to improve my skill and earn a higher salary.

Keep steadily in mind that faith in this principle is of first importance: Believe, then declare, then accept; all of this activates the realm of Cause — Law. Then act accordingly, for this is your active work in the objective realm of experience. Now *faith without works is dead.*

# CHAPTER IX

## SPIRITUAL GROWTH

THERE IS SOMETHING within us all which constantly pushes us forward, which demands continued progress.

Inertia may hinder our paying much attention to this inner urge, but it is always there. It is what keeps us going ahead, sometimes almost against our will. It is an inherent quality of man and asserts itself whether we welcome it or not, because it is what *we are*, demanding expression. Made in the image and likeness of the Father, one cannot accept stagnation; something protests against it. We must be moving forward into a higher and more satisfying spiritual stature. This "divine discontent" is a factor in our very make-up, and unless we are following its promptings we are not happy. We cannot get away from it because it is a part of our nature.

We are well aware of the fact that many people seem to have disregarded the important matter of spiritual growth, and, insofar as can be seen, are going down instead of up. But this may be entirely aside from the point; we do not know their inner experiences, their thoughts, nor hopes, nor longings. We do not know just where they are in spiritual awareness, nor how much they had to overcome in order to get even that far. Even though we may have known them from childhood, still we cannot really know their background in all its details. Because of this we cannot possibly know what their efforts toward growth really are. It is not our place to judge them. We have all we can do to look after our own unfoldment, and that is something for which we are specifically responsible.

## DOMINION OF THE BODY

It is encouraging to realize that your very nature is such

as to keep you growing, and also to provide the instrument through which that growth is accomplished. You have a physical body, a complex emotional nature, and an intellect. These three phases of your nature are so closely interrelated, and they react so definitely upon each other, that you have a triple set of capacities to be utilized in the process of advancement.

You are better acquainted with the nature of your physical body than with your emotions and mind, and it is well to begin with it. The body is the house in which, for the present, you are living and you need to keep it in good repair by a right mental attitude toward it, experiences, and people. Your body is entitled to your respect. "Know ye not that your body is the temple of the Holy [Spirit] . . . ?"

The body is acted upon by the emotions, and is particularly responsive to your emotional states. If you are sad, discouraged, gloomy, worried, or fearful — all of which are unwholesome emotions — your body immediately reflects that unwholesomeness and your state of health is lowered. The word "health" is simply the modern expression of the Old English "wholth," meaning wholeness. If you are not healthy emotionally, you cannot be in good health physically. Either will reflect the condition of the other, that which is predominant at the time. To keep the body in the best state of wholeness is of paramount importance.

## AN ATMOSPHERE OF HEALTH

We know now that there is such a close relationship between the body and the emotions that we learn to build bodily health through emotional health. Time ought to be given daily to such building. It is especially wise to faithfully keep in mind such expressions as these:

"I am filled with the Life and Love of God."

"I am strong and vibrant."

"God-Life surges through my entire body."

"I function normally, wholesomely, and effectively."

"The Power and Perfection of God flow through me constantly and keep me in superb health."

"I rejoice in physical wholeness."

When such statements are made with exuberant happiness, they carry a thrill of joy to every part of the body. They create and maintain that atmosphere of health in which new cells are created and in which they function. The good feeling which attends such statements becomes an "associated attitude" in the body, which persisted in becomes a habit carrying with it the power to continually reproduce itself.

This is very important because everyone sometimes finds himself below par physically and needs something to bring him back to normalcy. One of the best things you can do is to practice the use of such assertions. And also practice the appearance of a healthy body, such as the expanded chest, the erect posture, the free and easy carriage — all indicating good physical condition. They will become so associated with the positive and affirmative statements you make that they literally go together. Merely to begin repeating one of the statements will at once tend to reproduce the associated good physical condition. These "automatic reflexes" are wholesome parts of your endeavor. They cost you nothing in cash; they occupy only a minimum amount of time; they are pleasant to do, and they bring excellent results.

## RIGHT EMOTIONAL CONTROL

Good health, which is one of the results of such endeavor, is an important factor in the development of a fine personality; it shows that you have learned emotional control. We found that a good personality brings friendships, happiness, success, and prosperity. These are all of much interest to you. You want them. Now you see that they are directly tied up with the condition of your body; that they are largely the result of your emotions, and that your personal, social, and business success are all intertwined with this matter of emotional control. The relationships are so intimate and close that you cannot consider one without the other.

You need, of course, to train yourself steadily in the development of all those fine qualities which are positive, helpful, creative, and God-like.

Again we see that all phases of your nature cooperate. Right thinking brings right control over the emotions. When you feel well physically, you are happier. You also know that when you are happy you can keep your mind more easily attuned to what you want to be thinking. So, we also find that the condition of the body affects the quality of our thinking. When we use our intellect according to its *real* nature, we think clearly, logically, effectively, and have a vastly better perspective. We see things, conditions, events, and people in their right proportions. Through such thinking our good thoughts become things. When you recognize these fundamental facts and understand the threefold nature of yourself better you can use your creative thought to bring to pass those deep desires of your heart which mean so much to you.

## YOU CHANGE YOUR ENVIRONMENT

By means of such thinking you change your environment. For one thing, you have a higher appraisal of people and surroundings. You more clearly see the good in them, and much which before may have been hidden. There is a reaction to this appraisal! This is something you can easily prove for yourself and, incidentally, it is something you ought to be proving every day. When you think well of someone and especially when you express that approval, you immediately set a standard for him to which he tries to measure up. It is the quickest way to bring out the desired good qualities in any person.

Your environment consists of "things," as well as people, but your appreciation and approval of all that is good, even in things, will at least sustain their desirable qualities in your consciousness, thus making you happier. In addition, it will almost surely bring to mind something you can do to add to the appearance, condition, or usefulness of those same things, thus further increasing their desirability. Yes, thought does change environment.

## SPIRITUAL REALIZATION

Affirmative thinking makes it possible for you to work out your plans. This is so important that you can never afford to let negation interfere. Your thought must contain the best, because you do want to bring your good to fruition in the best possible way. When you are free from the negation of emotional conflict the mind becomes a clear, pure channel through which God-Wisdom flows, and there is created for you the good you desire. That is what is needed if you are to be successful. Then, too, the ability to think without the interference of negative feelings is necessary to the unfoldment of that deeper spiritual realization which is your highest aspiration. This is something you cannot neglect! Such realization is an unfoldment eminently deeper than intellectual accomplishment. It is such a conscious unifying of self with the Father that one is aware of a complete oneness. This is an experience one may not be able to put into words, but nevertheless it is so real that no one who experiences it can ever dispute it. It is what all mankind has forever sought, because it is the inherent nature of man, eventually, to find his true relationship to God — a son of God.

Clear thinking, health, happiness, friendships, and prosperity are all important and worthy. They are steps on the stairway up which man climbs in his ascent in spiritual realization.

## AUTOMATIC RESULTS

Looked at another way, it is just as correct to say that spiritual realization is the basis of all these experiences. Attaining a high spiritual consciousness, which we call realization, man is automatically assured of all these other things. It is a rule that works both ways.

How shall all of this be brought about? That is the practical question for which you seek an answer.

From the first page of this book you have been reading the answer to that query. In a most simple way you learned how your mind is constituted; how it is an expression and activity of the Mind of God; how you can use the creative power of your mind, applying it to your daily experiences. Step by step you have had a steady growth of understanding, and learned how to put that understanding to work.

One idea thoroughly understood and put into practice is vastly more valuable than the reading of many books if nothing more were done about it. Wide reading in a new field is often very confusing. Get yourself so completely saturated with a few basic principles, first, that they are firmly established in your mind and built into your thinking as habit. You will then be ready for additional material. No one has ever yet reached the place where there is nothing further he should be studying in regard to this all-important matter of personal development.

## THE SINCERE DESIRE

*Prayer* is the second part of your procedure in the attainment of realization. Because of the rich heritage of associations and experiences surrounding the word prayer, it is one of the most powerful and beautiful in our language. There is something of a benediction in just the word itself. And still, too often, it is not rightly understood. If you think of prayer as simply asking God for what you want, pleading for comfort, for supplies, coaxing for His favors, you are sadly limiting the meaning of this wondrous word.

Prayer is the contact of man's mind with God-Mind, in a way that shall result in bringing to pass a desired good. It lifts man into an awareness of his relationship to the Father. That relationship implies all the rights of sonship. Sonship means the right to the use and enjoyment of the Father's abundant supplies, and these supplies are material, emotional, and spiritual. We know that the Father is the All-surrounding Spirit, which is everything. We know each is entitled to his own rich share of that abundance.

We have found that effective prayer is the cleansing of thought, perfect believing, clear affirmation, and right action; time spent in quietly knowing your right as a son of the One Father, realizing your privileges of sonship, and the giving of grateful thanks — all this is prayer.

No modern wording can improve upon the definition in Montgomery's fine old hymn which begins:

> *Prayer is the soul's sincere desire,*
> *Uttered or unexpressed;*
> *The motion of a hidden fire*
> *That trembles in the breast.*

For another and much older expression of it, we read in Job:

> *Thou shalt make thy prayer unto him, and he shall hear*
> *thee, and thou shalt pay thy vows. Thou shalt also decree*
> *a thing, and it shall be established unto thee: and the*
> *light shall shine upon thy ways.*

In the very heart of this statement we find perfect assurance. There is calm, complete trust! There is perfect knowing!

## ACCORDING TO YOUR FAITH

Are prayers answered? Yes, if they truly be prayers. To what degree do the answers correspond to the desired results? Jesus answers that again and again: "According to thy faith be it unto thee."

How shall we pray? Again Jesus gives explicit directions:

> *Enter into thy closet, and when thou hast shut thy door,*
> *pray to thy Father which is in secret; and thy Father,*
> *which seeth in secret, shall reward thee openly.*

Let us be careful about the word closet. A quiet room where one is alone provides a privacy which often is conducive to effective prayer. Free from all distraction, man and God may enter into free and unconstrained communication. *Closet*, however, means much more than a private room; it means a temporary shutting of the mind to all that might interfere with the act of prayer. It means a shutting of the door on all worries, anxieties, fears, and tensions — everything which might intrude and disrupt the direction of your thought.

You are keeping an appointment with God, securing instructions from your Father. You must not let anything interfere with that appointment. You have entered into the closet of your mind, you are alone with God. Your prayer is a personal experience, and "the Father which seeth in secret shall reward thee openly." Afterward you go about your day's activities free from all anxiety because the Father's Wisdom is functioning in and through you. From such communion you have found new strength, happiness, and guidance. The prayer-time experience has provided a sense of vitality and security. Your work can now progress only in the right way. Your affairs shall prosper. *Realization* is yours.

More than this, however, you must remember that this joy, satisfaction, and sense of oneness must be translated into action in your relations with others. The rich inner experience has to be carried over into an outer expression which gives joy, courage, help, or specific good of some kind to other people. To retain the value of this inner spiritual experience you must share it; express it in action. This is a necessity.

The three steps of *study*, *prayer*, and *realization* are spiritual aspects of your endeavor, but all your physical, emotional, and intellectual activities also have their share in bringing into your experience the desired good which, in this case, is the unfoldment of your inner spiritual nature.

# CHAPTER X

## "BETTER LIVING" — *NOW!*

IF ONE DECIDES TO FOLLOW a certain procedure he wants to know what the results will be. This is only reasonable. You have been reading about spiritual principles and some of the aspects have been discussed separately. But you want to know about the larger over-all relationship of spiritual principles and the life you live.

Man is richly repaid physically, materially, and spiritually when he adheres to the laws of infinite Mind.

Genesis tells us that man is made in the image and likeness of God, and this assertion is closely followed by words declaring his power over all other creations: "...and let them have dominion..."

One of the God-qualities which you inherit is the creative nature of your thought. You need to recognize and express this for good. It is only natural and right that you should do so; not by imposing your will on others, but by the proper direction of this God-given ability for the betterment of conditions, circumstances, health, and emotions. The phrase, "Man, know thyself," lays the foundation for using your Divine gift properly.

### SELF-CONTROL

Even in the daily affairs of managing a business or a group of workers — in leadership of any kind — no one is truly worthy of such responsibility unless he has first learned self-control. This is the first essential in the application of the innate ability with which he is equipped.

For practical purposes you want to make wise use of this creative ability by using it for your physical well-being. If you are ill, or in any way below what you consider par, it is ample evidence that something needs to be done. No one wants to be ill! This is when you should assert your dominion; you should use your authority and declare and affirm in prayer that bodily conditions now return to normal. It can be done, and it constitutes one of the great advancements of modern study in the mental-psychological-spiritual field.

Science of Mind teaches that because you are a part of the Infinite's Oneness you can declare your perfect physical condition and it will manifest. This is definite use of spiritual Law. Your thought, backed by faith and conviction, is the start of your experience of physical wholeness, which becomes manifest to the extent of your belief in it.

The fact and experience of illness is not denied, but you learn to see it for what it really is — the outpicturing of a belief, idea, or pattern of thought. It is but an effect, the result of a cause. It can be changed or discarded and in its place you may establish as cause, in the creative realm of Law, the opposite creative idea — that of perfect health. Whatever is firmly planted in your mind, in absolute belief, is acted upon by the Law of Mind and has to come forth in your world of experience.

## PHYSICAL HEALING

If bodily illness confronts you, do this at least twice a day: Get as comfortable as you can, releasing all tension. Resolve that at least for a few minutes you will forget the bodily discomfort, the pain, the fever, or any other symptom which distresses you. Try to let go — to relax — all over, so that all tenseness disappears from your body. Close your eyes and know that your body is the house in which God dwells, that God is in you as you, that God is what you are. Then quietly, very slowly, with ample time for a deep realization of every word, say:

> There is One Life, that Life is God, that Life is perfect, that Life is my life now. My body is a manifestation of the living Spirit. It is created and sustained by the One Presence and the One Power. That Power is flowing in

*and through me now, animating every organ, every action, and every function of my physical being. There is perfect circulation, perfect assimilation, and perfect elimination. There is no congestion, no confusion, and no inaction. I am One with the infinite rhythm of Life which flows through me in love, in harmony, and in peace. There is no fear, no doubt, and no uncertainty in my mind. I am letting that Life which is perfect flow through me. It is my life now. There is One Life, that Life is God, that Life is perfect, that Life is my life now.*

## CONVINCE YOURSELF OF YOUR PERFECTION

You will notice that here no particular discomfort was named. You have not asked for anything. You have been trying to *realize* what you already *are*. This or a similar meditation should be used often during any period of illness. The big job you have to do is to *convince yourself* of your natural perfection. When all negation is wiped out of your consciousness and you feel that you are a specific part of the Infinite, a child of the One Father, with His qualities, you have then planted the idea of health in your mind and it will come forth in your body. This is what effective meditation or prayer does.

To bring healing to pass is, indeed, exercising your rightful dominion over your state of health.

## FINANCES

The desire to have direction over one's financial affairs is of great importance and value to many. All that has to be done is to examine once again the basic principle. It covers all our needs. The requirement is that you understand and obey the Law of infinite Mind. Whatever you believingly declare into Mind, and on which you act accordingly, is manifest in your affairs. Are you in need of money right now? Then let your meditation follow along these lines:

First of all, "enter into the closet" of your mind, the quiet, private place of your consciousness. Forget about your needs. Make yourself comfortable. Know that you are going to talk things over with your Senior Partner. You can trust Him, so let your mind be at peace. Lay aside your worries. Spend a few minutes thinking about the many blessing you already have — just the simple things of life — and name some of them and give thanks for them. Be truly grateful for them and say so! Remain in perfect quietness, and speaking your word softly, trustfully, and happily, use such expressions as these:

*Father, I am looking to You, as Senior Partner in my business affairs, for the guidance I need. I know that I am led to see and do what is right so that I am supplied with money for my every good need.*

*I now declare that right contacts are established, right influences are set into motion, and right activities are started so that my abundance becomes manifest. I declare there is right action in regard to all my affairs.*

*I know that the Universe responds to my believing word and that right results and rewards are mine. I am guided so that I see the right people, say and do the right things, give the right kind of service, and make myself valuable to others. Money to meet my every good requirement is now mine.*

*I live wholesomely and efficiently, and give generously. I know that abundant funds for doing so are now mine, and they come to me in exactly the right way.*

*I am grateful for this abundant supply; I give sincere thanks for it. I have decreed it and it is established unto me. I use it freely in the service of God and man, knowing that as it goes out in every way and in loving helpfulness to others, it is constantly being blessed, and that further funds will take its place as fast as needed.*

*Now I go out and "act accordingly." I express the attitude of abundance. I feel and look prosperous. I believe in my prosperity. And so I prosper.*

## EMPLOYMENT

If this meditation is used for the purpose of finding employment, it would be well to think of God as the great Business Manager who knows just where to send you for right contacts. If it is used for the improvement of your present business, take ample time to assert that new activity is now being manifest; that you are finding new ways to make your business more productive and, especially, that methods and ways of greater service come to your mind so that the business will become of more value to others. The Senior Partner in your business life can always supply you with the right plans, if you believingly decree and accept that it shall be so.

Your increased prosperity will probably involve a number of other people, their thinking, influence, cooperation, and perhaps actual activity. But you do not need to know who or where they are. Your Senior Partner will look after that for you. You have dominion over your business affairs just to the degree you believe you have, and act accordingly.

## A NEW IDEA

Sometimes a situation arises wherein you need an entirely new idea, and you have no way of knowing what it ought to be. In that case there is no specific *thing* to claim, only an *idea*; but claiming an idea, even when you do not know what it ought to be, is just as specific as though you were claiming quick shipment of goods, a position, money with which to buy a house, or anything else.

If this vague something — some idea — be such that it would solve your difficulties, accept it. Then the central part of your creative prayer-time might be worded something like this:

> *Father, as my Business Guide and Counselor, I know You are supplying me with exactly the right idea so that I can meet all requirements. I am grateful that even*

*when I do not know the specific idea I need, Your All-wise Mind does know.*

*I shall not permit myself to be worried or hurried about any new plan. I now accept the idea I need and the wisdom to handle all the details intelligently and successfully. The right idea becomes known to me. I accept it this moment.*

*At the right time it is presented to me and I shall recognize it. But, right now, this instant, I know it is already mine. I accept it thankfully and know I have the ability to carry it out faithfully, happily, enthusiastically, knowing that it shall succeed richly.*

*I do my part as a worthy Junior Partner in making life a success.*

This experience of accepting an idea when you have no information whatsoever as to what it ought to be, is one of the most satisfying you can ever have. Assure yourself over and over that your prayer is fulfilled. Don't worry if days and days go by without there seeming to be any response. You may be sure that the right developments are taking place. Your affairs are rightly being attended to. Steps are in progress to bring your new idea to you, together with the necessary knowledge and plans for its complete fulfillment. Be still, and wait. Believe. Accept.

## THE DETAILS WILL COME

Then some day, all of a sudden, perhaps when your mind is busy with something entirely different, even some trivial little matter, there will come a flash of inspiration and *you will know* that the idea has come!

At first it is quite likely you will see no possible way in which it could be carried out. That does not matter in the least. When God supplies an idea He is wise enough to furnish the plan for it. Give happy, sincere thanks for the idea; accept it; know it is the right one. Don't listen to the objections that will immediately come to mind. They will be good sensible ones, too, insofar as you know, but they can't compare with God-Wisdom. So when an idea comes from God, through the intuition, don't be so foolish as to let old concepts interfere with it. And without any anxiety, or sense of haste, you accept — in perfect confidence — the details of the plan by which your idea can be carried out. *They will come!*

You will, of course, go about every activity which would promote your idea, and don't push things. God's time is the right time. Everything will be made plain for you; your Partnership will continue to be a success. The Father furnishes the ideas, plans, inspiration, and courage as you are receptive to them. You, the son, carry out those plans by doing the work. The idea is the Father's. Your responsibility is to go about your work happily and successfully.

You can have dominion over your business affairs.

## SPIRITUAL DOMINION

What is spiritual dominion? Is it not already included in these simple everyday experiences and activities? Yes, and no. Everything is Spirit. We need always to keep that in mind. The results we have discussed are Spirit manifest in the tangible affairs of life, brought to pass through spiritual Law. If you have applied the basic principles to the commonplace activities of daily living, they will work with precision.

Complete spiritual dominion, however, implies something more difficult to explain because it is an inner personal experience. It is a state of awareness that man achieves as he completely accepts in himself the Father's Nature, and knows that he, too, is a part of Spirit, and therefore at one with the Father. Then he can say, as did Jesus, "I and the Father are one."

When man has a deep inner feeling that nothing separates him from God, he senses a great flood of satisfaction, peace, strength, and freedom which could never come to anyone except to him who had *chosen* to advance into a greater spiritual awareness. Remember that to go beyond the peak of your present growth demands that you choose to do so.

Little by little, as you advance, you come into a greater experience of spiritual awareness which is your natural right. Then you grow into ever greater spiritual dominion. Spiritual growth is the essence and beautiful Action of Life Itself. This is eminently important and is the ultimate reward which reflects in your abilities and activities of daily living.

In conclusion, remember that as you grow in knowledge of God, in spiritual awareness — which is every man's goal — you come to an intelligent understanding of spiritual Law and how to use It. And through the creative action of your thought as prayer you may realize and experience your every good desire.

*And God said ... let them have dominion ...*

# APPENDIX

## A SCIENCE OF RELIGION AND A
## RELIGION OF SCIENCE

THERE ARE THREE general classifications of knowledge, namely, science, philosophy, and religion. By science we mean the organized knowledge of natural law and its application to life. By philosophy we mean the opinions one holds about the world, life, and reality. Although we generally speak of philosophy in relation to those statements which have been put down in writing by men whose opinions we respect, as a matter of fact philosophy is anybody's opinion about anything. By religion we mean any man's belief about his relationship to the invisible universe. Or, we might say, religion is a man's idea of God, or gods — of the ultimate reality.

It follows, then, that there are many philosophies and many religions, since in both instances they constitute opinions. But not so with science, for science is a knowledge of the laws of nature. We also speak of pure science and applied science. Pure science is a knowledge of principles, while applied science is the technique for using universal principles.

A scientist, in whatever field of investigation he may be engaged, is one who uses universal principles. Once a principle is discovered and the laws governing it are ascertained, he maintains absolute faith in that principle.

Science is not an investigation into the why, but into the how. The why of anything, that is, the reason for its being, science makes no attempt to answer. If it should shift its field from the knowledge of principles and facts into the field of inquiry as to why these principles exist, then science becomes a philosophy.

Today, many men of science are beginning to speculate on

scientific principles. And, as they do this their speculations fall into two generalized classifications, philosophically speaking. These speculations usually lead them either to a philosophic basis of materialism or to a philosophic basis of idealism.

Both the idealist and the materialist believe that the universe is a thing of intelligence. The only difference is that the materialist refuses to admit that the intelligence operating through the laws of nature is backed by or permeated with any form of consciousness; that is, the intelligence is merely a blind but intelligent force, a conglomeration of immutable laws of cause and effect with no element of consciousness, no sentiment, no feeling. He sees only blind force, but he sees blind force intelligently organized.

The idealist feels that back of and operating in and through the laws of nature there is volition and consciousness. He maintains that the manifestation of physical life upon this planet always is in accord with organized intelligence. He feels that organized intelligence can be accounted for only on the basis that there is an engineer as well as an engine.

There are, then, these two branches of philosophy — the idealistic and the materialistic. The idealist believes in consciousness, hence a Spiritual Universe, while the materialist does not. Naturally, the scientist who is philosophically a materialist believes in no God, no Spiritual Universe, and no consciousness in the universe which responds to man. He does not believe in the immortality of the individual soul, nor can he give any real meaning to life. He may be a humanitarian and a very good man, but his ultimate philosophy is: "Six feet under and all is over."

The scientist who feels that there is consciousness in the universe finds no difficulty in believing in God or in the universe as a spiritual system, permeated with a consciousness which responds to man. Therefore he believes in prayer, immortality, the value of faith, and feels there is a definite meaning to life. An increasing number of scientific men are taking this position.

The scientist who is a materialist has no religion unless it be one of humanitarianism, while the idealist can scarcely get along without some form of religious conviction.

But if the idealist is a scientific man, believing as he must that everything is governed by law, his religion cannot be superstitious. He cannot believe in a God who specializes on one person more than on another, or who esteems one person above another; nor can he believe that the laws of nature can be broken or modified through anyone's prayer or faith. Therefore the scientific mind which is at the same time idealistic believes that the universe is not only intelligent, but that it is also consciousness, and will be satisfied with no religious concepts which contradict reason, common sense, and a cosmos of law and order.[1]

When the early discoveries of science refuted ancient superstitions and proved that this world was not the center of the universe, that it was round and not flat, the faith which many people had began to wane. The ancient shibboleths, dogmas, and superstitions could no longer be held valid for intelligent men, and formalized religion began to lose its hold on the inquiring scientific mind. Materialism was in the ascendency.

However, today we find increasing numbers of scientific men emerging from that age of materialism. This is due to the fact that modern science has not theoretically been able to resolve the material universe into purely mechanical energy, but has discovered that the smallest particles which it supposes to exist exercise a sort of volition, which of course leaves room for freedom.[2] Once you establish freedom and volition as an operating factor in connection with the energy which becomes form,[3] then you have established a universe of consciousness. And once you establish a universe of consciousness you establish the possibility of communion, and arrive at a logical basis for faith, prayer, the religious and the mystical life.

There has been a tremendous growth of knowledge which has taken place in the world in the last few hundred years. However, the vast majority of people have given but little thought to the implications involved. To most people religion has been either superstitiously entertained — and no doubt with great benefit to those who believed in it — or else it was rejected.

Today, however, there is a certain and rather swift return to spiritual convictions. These new, vital and dynamic spiritual concepts have placed firm foundations beneath man's innate religious tendency, firm foundations which scientific men need not reject and which the unscientific man may accept without superstition.[4]

This is what is meant when we speak of a scientific religion. We do not mean that religion is reduced to coldness, without sentiment or feeling, but rather that law and order are added to the sentiment and the feeling. We have a perfect right to speak of a scientific religion or a religion of science. But upon what could such a scientific religion be based? It could only be based upon the principle of Mind, of Intelligence and Consciousness, which many outstanding scientists today assert is the ultimate and fundamental reality.

Science, in affirming consciousness in the universe, that is, a spiritual Presence and an Intelligence, also affirms that the individual's consciousness is of similar nature.[5] Therefore a scientific religion does not exclude what we call prayer or communion even though it lays greater stress on communion than on petition. For instance, a scientific religion could not believe that man's petitions to God can change the natural order of the universe or reverse the laws of nature.

However, prayer now becomes the communion of the lesser with the greater, which makes it possible for man, not to reverse natural law but to reverse his position in it in such a way that bondage becomes freedom.[6]

We might speak of a pure religious science as we would speak of a pure natural science, which means the study of natural causes. We might speak of pure religious science as that branch of science which studies the natural principles; the nature of Mind and Consciousness. Then we could think of applied religious science as the application of this principle to human needs for practical purposes, and this is where one encounters the study of the nature of prayer, of faith, and of mental actions and reactions.

In the use of faith, prayer, communion, or spiritual treatment, one would be applying the principles of Mind, Spirit, Intelligence, Consciousness, and Law and Order to the persistent problems of everyday life. He would, then, be more than a theoretical religionist; he would have an applied and a practical religion.

This is exactly what we mean when we speak of a science of religion and a religion of science, for we are using this term in its broadest sense. We are using the term religion from the standpoint of universal religion, including all religious beliefs — Christian, Buddhist, Mohammedan, or any other faith — and we are thinking of prayer, communion, and the laws of consciousness as applied to any and all people. In short, we are universalizing the Principle which by nature is universal. Thus each religion approaches the same God, and must basically believe in the same God. But a scientific religion cannot believe in any concept of God which denies a universe of law and order, or which attempts to exclude anyone from its benefits.

It would be unscientific as well as irrational to believe that God, or the Supreme Intelligence, holds one man in higher esteem than another. For as the Bible so truthfully and boldly declares: "And let him that is athirst come. And whosoever will, let him take the water of life freely."

One comes to agree with Robert Browning that "all's love, yet all's law," and that there is an impersonal Law as well as a personal relationship to the Spirit. This Law exists for all, like the laws of mathematics or any other natural law, but the personal relationship is personified through each at the level of his consciousness, at the level of his comprehension of what God means to him.

Intelligence and reason must be the rules of thought, and

God must be accessible to all on equal terms. The scientific religionist could not believe in miracles, but he would not deny the power of spiritual thought. Rather he would think that the so-called miracles performed as a result of spiritual faith have been in accord with natural law and cosmic order, and that they could be reproduced at will. That which the illumined have experienced and that which men of great spiritual power have proved, the scientific religionist feels should be deliberately used in everyday life.

To the individual believing there is a Principle, Intelligence, or Consciousness governing all things, there comes a feeling that he understands the laws, or at least some of the laws, of this Principle; hence he feels that it is intensely sane, as well as humanly practical, to apply faith, consciousness, and spiritual conviction to the solution of human problems. This is what is meant by spiritual mind treatment.

Spiritual mind treatment is based on the belief or the theory, which we now feel has a sound basis, that there is a Principle of Intelligence in the universe which is not only creative, giving rise to objective form, but It is immediately responsive to our consciousness, and, being universal It is omnipresent, and being omnipresent It is not only where we are but It is what we are.' Hence the scientific religionist feels that he understands what Jesus meant when he said: "The words that I speak unto you I speak not of myself, but the Father, that dwelleth in me, he doeth the works."

Just as all pure science, before it can be of any use to humanity, must pass into applied science, so pure religious concepts, before they can have a practical application, must pass into applied religion. And it is the application of religion to the solution of our problems which we may speak of as demonstrating the Principle.

What, then, are the pure and applied aspects of this Principle? The basis or pure concept is that there is an Absolute Intelligence in the universe — one, undivided, birthless, deathless, changeless Reality. Since no one made God and since God did not make Himself, that which was, is, and is to be, will remain.

According to our first axiom that God is all there is, there is the implication that there is nothing else beside Him. Hence the entire manifestation of Life is an evolution or an unfoldment of form from that which is formless and eternal. This intelligent Cause, this undifferentiated and undistributed God-Principle, one and complete within Itself, is the source from which all action proceeds and in which all creation takes place.

At this point one may logically hold the belief, the opinion, or the certainty that God as man, in man, is man; that when man makes a proclamation it is still God proclaiming, but, at the level of man's consciousness. Therefore the cosmos is reflected in, or manifested by or through, the individual. One cannot say, "Why is man?" any more than one can say, "Why is God?" Intelligence exists and man interprets It. Therefore man is Its mouthpiece; man is a personification of the Infinite, governed by the same laws. But man is more than law; he is consciousness.

The application of the principles of such a science of religion to our everyday problems is just as necessary as that there must be a practical application of the theories of any science for them to be of value. It is not enough merely to speculate or philosophize. It is certainly not enough to abstract our thought and announce an Infinite, for the Infinite can never at any time mean more to us than the use we make of It. Just as electricity can never mean more to us than the use we make of it. This is true of any and all principles of nature.

If there is an infinite Creative Intelligence which makes things out of Itself by Itself becoming the thing that It makes, and if man exists and is conscious, then the Creative Genius of this Universal Mind is also the creative genius of Its individualization, which we call man.

From the above stated propositions intelligence cannot escape, correct induction and deduction cannot escape. Thus, most of the great intellectual geniuses who have ever lived have proclaimed these truths, each in his own tongue, in his own way, in his own day, for his own age. Many believe that Jesus proclaimed them for all ages since he was so universal in his concepts.

Such a way of thinking does not belong to any sect, to any group, to any class, and most certainly not to any person. There is no claim to special revelation; rather, for this particular system of thought there have been gathered together facts from all ages and all people, from all philosophies and religions. And using practical methods, which any other scientific research would use, it is able to, and does, present a Science of Mind with a message of freedom.

*This Appendix is a reprint of an article from the comprehensive extension Study Course in The Science of Mind which consists of forty-eight lessons and covers a full year of study.*

---

[1] *"Religion and natural science are fighting a joint battle in an incessant, never relaxing crusade against skepticism and against dogmatism, against disbelief and against superstition, and the rallying cry in this crusade has always been, and always will be: 'On to God!' "*—MAX PLANCK

[2] *Heisenberg's Theory of Indeterminacy.*

[3] *Einstein's theory of the equivalence of energy and mass.*

[4] *"The idea that God . . . is not a being of caprice and whim, as had been the case in all the main body of thinking of the ancient world, but is instead a God who rules through law . . . That idea has made modern science and it is unquestionably the foundation of modern civilization."*—ROBERT A. MILLIKAN

[5] *. . . That consciousness is a singular of which the plural is unknown; that there is only one thing and that, which seems to be a plurality, is merely a series of different aspects of this one thing."*—ERWIN SCHRODINGER

[6] *"Prayer and propitiation may still influence the course of physical phenomena when directed to these centers."*—SIR ARTHUR EDDINGTON

[7] *"We discover that the universe shows evidence of a designing or controlling power that has something in common with our own individual minds."*—SIR JAMES JEANS